# Cambridge Elements

Elements in Applied Linguistics
edited by
Li Wei
*University College London*
Zhu Hua
*University College London*

# TRANSLANGUAGING IN CLASSROOM DISCOURSE

Kevin W. H. Tai
*The University of Hong Kong*

## CAMBRIDGE
## UNIVERSITY PRESS

Shaftesbury Road, Cambridge CB2 8EA, United Kingdom

One Liberty Plaza, 20th Floor, New York, NY 10006, USA

477 Williamstown Road, Port Melbourne, VIC 3207, Australia

314–321, 3rd Floor, Plot 3, Splendor Forum, Jasola District Centre,
New Delhi – 110025, India

Cambridge University Press is part of Cambridge University Press & Assessment,
a department of the University of Cambridge.

We share the University's mission to contribute to society through the pursuit of
education, learning and research at the highest international levels of excellence.

www.cambridge.org
Information on this title: www.cambridge.org/9781009660600
DOI: 10.1017/9781009660624

© Kevin W. H. Tai 2026

This publication is in copyright. Subject to statutory exception and to the provisions
of relevant collective licensing agreements, no reproduction of any part may take
place without the written permission of Cambridge University Press & Assessment.

When citing this work, please include a reference to the DOI 10.1017/9781009660624

First published 2026

A catalogue record for this publication is available from the British Library

A Cataloging-in-Publication data record for this Element is available from the Library
of Congress

ISBN 978-1-009-66060-0 Hardback
ISBN 978-1-009-66057-0 Paperback
ISSN 2633-5069 (online)
ISSN 2633-5050 (print)

Cambridge University Press & Assessment has no responsibility for the persistence
or accuracy of URLs for external or third-party internet websites referred to in this
publication and does not guarantee that any content on such websites is, or will remain,
accurate or appropriate.

For EU product safety concerns, contact us at Calle de José Abascal, 56, 1°, 28003
Madrid, Spain, or email eugpsr@cambridge.org

# Translanguaging in Classroom Discourse

Elements in Applied Linguistics

DOI: 10.1017/9781009660624
First published online: March 2026

Kevin W. H. Tai
*The University of Hong Kong*

Author for correspondence: Kevin W. H. Tai, kevin.tai@hku.hk

**Abstract:** This Element aims to provide evidence-based, research-informed applications of translanguaging pedagogies across various multilingual classroom contexts. By offering both theoretical implications and specific examples of translanguaging in action, the Element aims to help educators to implement translanguaging pedagogy that challenges monolingual norms in educational institutions. The Element also explores new theoretical notions derived from translanguaging, such as translanguaging sub-spaces, transpositioning, transknowledging, transmodalities, transculturing, transbordering, transsemiotising, and transprogramming. Additionally, it critically examines various methodological approaches for researching translanguaging in classroom settings, proposing a combination of Multimodal Conversation Analysis and Interpretative Phenomenological Analysis to capture the complexity of classroom translanguaging practices. This Element concludes by asserting that adopting a translanguaging perspective is an ethical and pedagogical imperative, providing the essential theoretical and methodological frameworks for creating equitable, inclusive, and transformative multilingual learning environments.

This Element also has a video abstract: www.cambridge.org/Kevin

**Keywords:** translanguaging, classroom discourse, language policy and medium of instruction policy, multilingual education, translanguaging space

© Kevin W. H. Tai 2026

ISBNs: 9781009660600 (HB), 9781009660570 (PB), 9781009660624 (OC)
ISSNs: 2633-5069 (online), 2633-5050 (print)

# Contents

1 Introduction: Conceptualization of the Notion of Translanguaging    1

2 Translanguaging Practices in Multilingual Classrooms    13

3 Expanding the Conceptualization of Translanguaging: Theoretical Development and Implications for Pedagogy    36

4 Researching Translanguaging in Classroom Interactions    49

5 Conclusion    66

References    78

# 1 Introduction: Conceptualization of the Notion of Translanguaging

As classrooms increasingly feature students from diverse linguistic backgrounds, it has become crucial to re-evaluate teaching methods to ensure fair and inclusive learning experiences for multilingual students. Conventional language teaching techniques, such as task-based language teaching (e.g., East and Wang, 2025 and communicative language teaching (Anderson, 2024), which typically emphasize solely on written and verbal communication in the target language, often fail to acknowledge the valuable linguistic and meaning-making resources that multilingual students contribute. These students will bring with them 'funds of knowledge' which are 'the historically accumulated and culturally developed bodies of knowledge and skills essential for households and individual functioning and wellbeing' (Moll et al., 1992, p. 133). Both the teacher and students can benefit from incorporating these funds of knowledge in the classroom, not only to promote inclusivity but also for promoting meaning-making and identity exploration, which are vital aspects of education that are often overlooked (Li, 2014). Research conducted by Moll et al. (1992) demonstrated that when teachers relinquish their positions as experts and adopt a new role as collaborative learners, they can develop a unique and deeper understanding of the lived experiences and knowledge of the students and their families. It is argued that when teachers capitalize on the diverse funds of knowledge, they can transform the quality of classroom interaction, which goes beyond the traditional, repetitive, and memorization-based instruction that students commonly encounter in schools. Consequently, translanguaging pedagogy has been introduced as a transformative approach in language education (García and Li, 2014; Tai, 2024a). A translanguaging pedagogy, unlike pedagogical translanguaging, does not ask multilinguals to keep their named languages compartmentalized as separate mental-linguistic systems or to use one language as a tool to learn another. Instead, a translanguaging pedagogy invites multilinguals to draw on their entire multilingual and semiotic repertoire – all their meaning-making resources – and to select the features and modes that best serve how they construct their worlds and understandings (Li, 2024).

Translanguaging describes how speakers draw on the full breadth of their linguistic and semiotic resources to make meaning (Li, 2018; Tai, 2023). This perspective contrasts with code-switching, which treats named languages as structurally and functionally distinct and assigns them different pedagogical roles in classrooms. Rather than simply alternating or translating between languages, translanguaging softens the boundaries among named languages and across modalities such as speech, signing, and gesture. Much code-switching research assumes that the sets of forms labelled as languages are also separate in cognition, defining a multilingual as someone who knows two or more named languages (e.g., Han et al., 2022). In doing so, it accepts the traditional, politically determined borders of 'languages' (e.g., English, French). Yet naming languages is a political act; whether a set of linguistic features is officially recognized depends on the community's socio-economic, military, and religious power (Li, 2018). Translanguaging challenges these borders, arguing that in speakers' minds, resources are not neatly segmented; the boundaries are fluid and permeable.

The concept of translanguaging has garnered significant attention in the field of Applied Linguistics, offering researchers and educators a new perspective on understanding language and better supporting multilingual learners in culturally and linguistically affirming, justice-oriented ways. Recently, scholars have used translanguaging as an analytical framework to explore various interactional phenomena in multilingual classrooms, including transpositioning (Li and Lee, 2024; Tai, 2025a; Tai and Lee, 2024), transmodalities (Hawkins, 2018), transknowledging (Heugh, 2021), and transprogramming (Tai, 2024a). Despite the increasing body of research on translanguaging, teachers and practitioners often struggle to effectively and strategically implement and maintain translanguaging pedagogical practices in their classrooms (Sah and Li, 2022; Mendoza et al., 2023; Wong and Tai, 2023).

To bridge the gap between research and practice, this Element provides evidence-based, research-informed applications of translanguaging pedagogies across various multilingual classroom contexts. These include English as a First Language classrooms, English as an Additional Language (EAL) classrooms, English Medium Instruction (EMI) or Content and Language Integrated Learning (CLIL) classrooms, Information Technology classrooms, virtual language learning environments, and Chinese as an Additional Language (CAL) classrooms. By presenting both theoretical insights and concrete examples of translanguaging in practice, this Element encourages and empowers teachers and educators to implement translanguaging pedagogy in their classrooms, thereby challenging monolingual norms within educational institutions. Additionally, this Element is well-suited for teacher education programmes as an introductory text to support teachers' understanding and independent development of translanguaging pedagogy tailored to their unique teaching contexts.

This section will provide an overview of the conceptualization of translanguaging, beginning with its foundation as a pedagogical resource, highlighting the need to maximize learners' potential by encouraging the use of their entire communicative repertoire in an integrated, dynamic, and fluid manner. It distinguishes between 'pedagogical translanguaging' – a theoretical and instructional approach to improve language and content competences using learners' full linguistic repertoire – and 'translanguaging pedagogy', which focuses on language practices for inclusion and social justice. Next, the section discusses translanguaging as a practical theory of language, which raises questions beyond language education, in academic fields including human cognition and communication. Finally, the section concludes with a discussion on transforming the classroom into a translanguaging space. This concept envisions the classroom as a dynamic environment where multilingual, multimodal, multisemiotic, and multi-sensory resources are orchestrated to create meaning. It also considers translanguaging as an analytical perspective to understand multilingual classrooms as a translanguaging space.

## 1.1 Translanguaging as a Pedagogical Resource

The term *trawsieithu*, initially introduced by Cen Williams (1994), promotes the concurrent use of English and Welsh in classrooms to enhance teaching and learning outcomes. Later, Baker (2001) translated the term into English as 'translanguaging', aiming to describe pedagogical approaches that leverage multiple language resources. In its original sense, translanguaging refers to the intentional, strategic planning of how the two languages are used in educational settings. This perspective was ground-breaking, as it challenged the monolingual mindset dominant in the Welsh education system, where bilingual communication in classrooms was often viewed as a challenge rather than a resource (Williams, 1994; Baker, 2001). As Williams (1996, p. 64) explained, 'translanguaging involves receiving information in one language (e.g., English) and using it in another (e.g., Welsh)'. The aim of this strategy is to strengthen both languages and deepen comprehension. For example, students might read and discuss a topic in one language and then write about it in another. Here, the shift between languages is purposeful and planned rather than random. Translanguaging not only helps learners grasp content more deeply but also uses the stronger language to support the development of the weaker one, fostering balanced bilingual growth. As Baker (2011, p. 290) highlights, 'teachers can allow students to use both languages in a planned, strategic, and developmental way to maximize their linguistic and cognitive abilities, reflecting the sociocultural nature of language in both content and process'. As Lewis et al. (2012) note, translanguaging offers scaffolding that can be gradually phased out as learners gain greater language proficiency. This understanding of translanguaging aligns with Vygotsky's (1962) Sociocultural Theory of learning, which can enrich bilingual classroom practices. The connection is not merely about support but about the very mechanism of learning. Specifically, translanguaging operationalizes three core tenets of Sociocultural Theory:

(1) The Zone of Proximal Development (ZPD): A learner's ZPD is the space between what they can do alone and what they can achieve with expert guidance. For a multilingual student, a monolingual task in their new language may be outside their independent ability. However, by strategically leveraging their entire linguistic and multimodal repertoire – using their stronger language to comprehend a complex text or brainstorm ideas – they, with their teacher or peers, create a 'bilingual ZPD'. The scaffolding is the essential vehicle that mediates understanding and propels them to a higher level of independent proficiency.

(2) Mediation through Psychological Tools: Sociocultural Theory posits that humans use 'tools' to mediate and master their mental processes. While a monolingual classroom treats only the target language as a valid tool, a translanguaging perspective recognizes multilinguals' full linguistic and semiotic repertoires as the ultimate mediating tool kit. Using a home language to draft an essay, translate a key concept, or co-construct knowledge in a group is not a deviation from learning; it is the fundamental cognitive process of learning. It allows multilinguals to internalize new knowledge and language by connecting it to their existing cognitive schemata.

(3) Social Interaction and Collaborative Dialogue: Learning, in Sociocultural Theory, is first social (between people) before it becomes psychological (within the individual). Translanguaging creates the conditions for rich, collaborative dialogue by removing the artificial constraint of a one-language-only or one-language-at-a-time policy. When students can use all their full repertoires to problem-solve, explain, and debate with peers and teachers, they engage in more profound and authentic social interactions. This collaborative talk, mediated by their full linguistic and multimodal resources, is what leads to the internalization of both content knowledge and new language forms (Rajendram, 2023).

It is important to highlight that the notion of translanguaging was initially developed as a perspective on language use, shifting the focus towards learning and meaning-making through the dynamic and integrated use of multiple languages across different modalities, rather than being a specific language teaching method. In essence, it is a learner-centred approach where teachers facilitate and encourage the flexible use of various languages to enhance understanding and strengthen students' abilities in both languages (Williams, 1994). As a pedagogy, translanguaging advocates for a transition from a focus on the medium of instruction to the medium of learning. This approach underscores the importance of respecting and maximizing learner agency, which includes enabling students to draw on their diverse communicative repertoires for meaning-making and fostering their multicompetence (García and Li, 2014; Cenoz and Gorter, 2021). Translanguaging challenges monolingual medium-of-instruction policies, whether in target-language-only second or foreign language learning, EMI, or one-language-at-a-time bilingual or multilingual education programs (Cenoz and Gorter, 2021). At its core, translanguaging scholarship focuses on bilingual and multilingual language users and their practices. It argues that learners achieve the best outcomes when they are given the freedom to flexibly use their full communicative repertoire, rather than being restricted to a single language or mode of communication.

It is crucial to distinguish between translanguaging as pedagogy (a broad pedagogical principle for social justice and learning) and pedagogical translanguaging (a specific set of instructional practices). While related, they operate at different levels of pedagogical application. The concept of pedagogical translanguaging, as proposed by Cenoz and Gorter (2021), is defined as 'planned by the teacher within the classroom and can involve using different languages for input and output or other intentional strategies that draw on students' full linguistic repertoires' (Cenoz, 2017, p. 194). Importantly, Cenoz and Gorter (2017) distinguished between pedagogical translanguaging and spontaneous translanguaging. Spontaneous translanguaging is unplanned, fluid, and discursive, typically occurring in natural settings, though it can be strategically leveraged for educational purposes. In contrast, pedagogical translanguaging is a deliberate instructional approach that integrates two or more languages. Initially applied in Welsh contexts, pedagogical translanguaging refers to planned teaching practices that utilize diverse linguistic resources and strategies to transcend language boundaries (Cenoz and Gorter, 2021). This approach extends the original concept of translanguaging by incorporating additional strategies to develop students' morphological, lexical, and textual awareness, while also activating their prior knowledge. The goal is for students to draw on their entire linguistic repertoire, behaving as multilinguals both when learning languages and when learning through different languages. By activating and building on students' prior knowledge, pedagogical translanguaging aims to improve learning outcomes, allowing students to notice similarities and differences between languages. This process enhances their metalinguistic awareness, particularly among multilingual speakers (Galante, 2020; Leonet et al., 2020). Research on minority language revitalization has explored how pedagogical translanguaging can support the maintenance and revitalization of vulnerable languages in educational settings (e.g., Cenoz and Gorter, 2017; Seals and Olsen-Reeder, 2020). Cenoz and

Gorter (2017) developed a framework of sustainable translanguaging, which argues that translanguaging can sustain minority languages if certain principles are applied. These include designing safe translanguaging spaces, creating a need to use minority languages through translanguaging, and enhancing learners' metalinguistic awareness. Seals and Olsen-Reeder's (2020) school-based ethnographies in New Zealand demonstrate how this framework provides a set of principles for researchers and teachers to collaboratively design tasks and activities that promote pedagogical translanguaging.

In contrast, translanguaging as pedagogy is a broader, more transformative pedagogical principle (Li, 2024). As Li (2024) explained, while pedagogical translanguaging emphasizes carefully planned practices that mobilize students' linguistic repertoires (Cenoz and Gorter, 2021), translanguaging as pedagogy goes further. A key distinction lies in the scope of resources they engage: pedagogical translanguaging is predominantly planned around linguistic resources, whereas translanguaging as pedagogy intentionally incorporates multimodal, semiotic, and cultural resources as fundamental to meaning-making. Translanguaging as pedagogy focuses on 'building on bilingual students' language practices flexibly to develop new understandings and new language practices' (García and Li, 2014, p. 233). It is not merely a method, but a stance that seeks to validate multilinguals' identity through actively encourage students to bring their personal experiences, perspectives, and voices into the classroom, restructure power dynamics in the classroom through positioning the teacher as a co-learner who leverages students' full linguistic, semiotic, and modal resources to construct knowledge collaboratively (Tai and Li, 2021a), and promote social justice through challenging monolingual biases by creating an inclusive environment where all communicative resources are valued.

Therefore, while pedagogical translanguaging provides the essential how – the specific, planned strategies for using multiple languages in instruction – translanguaging as pedagogy offers a guiding principle that invites teachers to enable learners to mobilize their full repertoires to learn and to encourage teachers and students to create a democratic, equitable, and cognitively empowering learning space (Li, 2024). This distinction highlights that translanguaging as pedagogy does not require teachers to be multilingual themselves, but rather calls for an open mindset that enables students to use their entire repertoire for meaning-making (García and Li, 2014).

## 1.2 Translanguaging as a Theory of Language

Beyond its educational applications, translanguaging has reshaped our understanding of language and communication. The emergence of translanguaging provides a unique opportunity to develop a theory of language and communication rooted in the everyday practices of bilingual and multilingual individuals. Translanguaging challenges the notion of named languages – such as English, Dutch, German, Cantonese, Mandarin, or Hakka – as socially constructed entities. Building on Cook's concept of multicompetence (see Cook and Li, 2016), it raises critical questions:

(1) Is language a separate and distinct module in the human mind, independent of other cognitive systems like memory, attention, and emotion?
(2) If the multilingual mind functions as a unified whole, where, if at all, do divisions between languages occur?
(3) If the human mind does not separate languages or distinguish between language and other cognitive systems, should research on bilingualism and multilingualism focus on how individuals use their diverse linguistic, cognitive, semiotic, and modal resources in social interactions, rather than on which or how many languages they know and use?

These questions are vital because they dismantle the monolingual bias that has long dominated linguistics, shifting the focus from the abstract systems of 'languages' to the lived reality of the multilingual speaker. This perspective directly informs Li's (2018, p. 18) proposal of translanguaging as a practical theory of language, which posits that:

(1) Multilinguals do not think in a single, politically named language, even when they are in a 'monolingual mode' and producing speech or text in one identifiable language for a specific period.
(2) Human thought extends beyond language, relying on a range of cognitive, semiotic, and modal resources, with conventional language (speech and writing) being just one component.

From a translanguaging perspective, a multilingual is someone who recognizes the political constructs of named languages, has learned some of their structural features, but possesses a Translanguaging Instinct (Li, 2016). This instinct transcends socially constructed languages and other semiotic systems, enabling individuals to leverage differences, discrepancies, inconsistencies, and ambiguities among them for meaning-making in social contexts. In this view, the multicompetent mind is not a collection of separate languages but an integrated ecosystem, and translanguaging is the natural expression of its underlying unity.

Furthermore, the theoretical foundations of translanguaging as a theory of language are shaped by scholarship on 'languaging' from two key perspectives: the sociocultural perspective and the ecological psychological perspective. As mentioned in Section 1, from the sociocultural viewpoint, translanguaging aligns with core ideas from Vygotsky's Sociocultural Theory, such as mediation and tools (Vygotsky, 1978). Swain (2006) has extensively argued that 'languaging serves to mediate cognition' (p. 97), highlighting how language functions as a vital tool in mediating learners' cognitive processes to solve problems and construct meaning during discussions. Swain (2006, p. 97) further explained that 'language acts as a vehicle through which thinking is articulated and transformed into an artefactual form'. This connects to the process of internalization, where learners externalize their thoughts through social interactions and then reflect on these externalizations to refine their understanding. Swain (2006, p. 98) concluded that 'languaging about language is one of the ways we learn language'. From this perspective, Swain views language learning as an ongoing process rather than a fixed outcome, emphasizing the negotiation and co-construction of meaning.

Complementing this, the ecological psychological perspective views languaging as a 'distributed and heterogeneous biocultural resource' that extends across individuals, environmental affordances, and cultural patterns (Thibault, 2011, p. 240). This perspective highlights that languaging 'operates across diverse spatiotemporal scales, ranging from the neural to the cultural' (Thibault, 2011, p. 210). Love's (1990) distinction between first-order language and second-order language challenges the traditional, or 'code view', of language, which focuses on identifying linguistic units like verbal patterns, morphosyntax, or lexicogrammar, while overlooking cognitive, affective, and bodily dimensions. A pivotal distinction in this school of thought is between first-order languaging and second-order language (Love, 1990).

Following Love's work, scholars, such as Thibault and Cowley, critiqued the code view and instead regard language as a second-order construct – a product of first-order activity, which is languaging itself (Thibault, 2011; Cowley, 2017). First-order languaging refers to 'the organization of processes on different scales that occur when individuals engage in conversation together', involving 'synchronized interindividual bodily dynamics on very short, rapid timescales, ranging from fractions of a second to milliseconds' (Thibault, 2011, p. 214). This suggests that during interaction, individuals 'enact, exploit, respond to, and attune to' each other's worlds (Thibault, 2011, p. 214). Thibault (2011) further explained that first-order languaging encompasses not only vocalization but also the coordination and synchronization of various bodily resources, along with extrabodily aspects of the situation.

In contrast, second-order language refers to the conventional understanding of language, where 'lexicogrammatical patterns act as attractors – future causes – that guide and constrain first-order languaging. These patterns are stabilized cultural constructs operating on longer, slower cultural timescales'

(Thibault, 2011, p. 216). Second-order language, such as verbal patterns, represents 'reified products of first-order languaging' (Thibault, 2017, p. 80) and plays a significant role in shaping overall languaging behaviour.

From an ecological psychological perspective, languaging is inherently dynamic, allowing individuals to attune to and focus on the immediate behaviours of their interlocutors. It is understood as 'an assemblage of diverse material, biological, semiotic, and cognitive properties and capacities that languaging agents orchestrate in real-time and across various timescales' (Thibault, 2017, p. 82). In essence, languaging emphasizes the concept of orchestration, which brings to the forefront elements such as 'feeling, experience, history, memory, subjectivity, and culture' (Li, 2018, p. 17), rather than adhering to rigid distinctions between linguistic, paralinguistic, and extralinguistic aspects of human communication. Translanguaging, therefore, can be understood as the practical orchestration of a person's entire linguistic and semiotic repertoires, grounded in the continuous, first-order activity of meaning-making that is central to both the sociocultural and ecological views of language.

As the concept has evolved into a theoretical framework, translanguaging incorporates a multimodal perspective, recognizing that individuals can draw on a broad repertoire of multimodal resources to create meaning. Li (2018) expanded the notion of translanguaging to include multilingual, multi-semiotic, multisensory, and multimodal practices that individuals use for thinking and expressing thoughts. In this way, translanguaging not only challenges traditional ideas of named languages but also extends beyond language in the conventional sense of speech and writing, which is just one of many communication tools (Li, 2022, 2024). This perspective has gained support in recent scholarly works (e.g., Zhu et al., 2017; Tai and Li, 2020; Ho, 2022; Mendoza et al., 2023; Tai, 2023), which explicitly highlight multimodality as a fundamental aspect of translanguaging. In other words, translanguaging encompasses a wide range of semiotic resources that individuals utilize in meaning-making, emphasizing the integration and coordination of various communicative modes (Li, 2022). This approach empowers multilingual speakers to construct knowledge through their diverse available resources, including linguistic elements such as words, sounds, and structures, as well as multimodal features like gestures and images (García and Li, 2014).

This multimodal dimension is not merely an addition but is deeply embedded in the core principles of translanguaging, as captured by the prefix 'trans-'. Li (2018) emphasized that the prefix 'trans-' in translanguaging captures three key dimensions:

(1) Transcending: Breaking down the boundaries between named languages and other cognitive and semiotic systems.

(2) Transformative: The capacity of translanguaging practices to transform not only learners' linguistic abilities but also their cognitive processes and identities.
(3) Transdisciplinary: Adopting an interdisciplinary approach to reimagine language, language learning, and language use across fields such as linguistics, psychology, sociology, and education.

Consequently, a translanguaging perspective necessitates that researchers and educators move beyond analysing speech and writing as separate codes. Instead, the focus must shift to multilingual individuals' ability to orchestrate their diverse linguistic, embodied, and multimodal resources to create new forms of expression and communication, thereby fully realizing the transcending, transformative, and transdisciplinary potential of their communicative practices.

## 1.3 Translanguaging as an Analytical and Methodological Perspective

In addition to serving as a pedagogy and a practical theory of language and communication, translanguaging has also emerged as an analytical perspective in Applied Linguistics research. This approach centres on bilingual and multilingual language use, prioritizing everyday translanguaging practices in its analysis. It does not privilege any specific communication mode or method over others when examining data (Li, 2022).

### 1.3.1 A Shift in Analytical Focus

A key aspect of this perspective is the emphasis on transcending boundaries between different forms of expression. Methodologically, adopting translanguaging as an analytical framework shifts the focus away from structural analyses that identify frequent and regular linguistic patterns. Instead of concentrating on high-frequency and regular patterns, as seen in traditional research on language variation and change (e.g., Cheshire and Fox, 2009) or Conversation Analysis studies that examine sequential patterns in social interactions (e.g., Tai and Brandt, 2018; Tai and Khabbazbashi, 2019a, 2019b), the translanguaging perspective encourages researchers to explore how language users break boundaries between named languages and non-linguistic semiotic systems during specific moments of classroom interaction (Li, 2011). This approach highlights the spontaneity and transient nature of social interactions (Li, 2020), shedding light on the creative and critical practices of multilingual individuals in social contexts. In essence, it enables researchers to uncover how individuals creatively leverage the affordances of various social and linguistic resources to go beyond the constraints of named languages and sociocultural norms.

### 1.3.2 Core Methodological Principles

From this methodological perspective, researchers are encouraged to examine how individuals dynamically orchestrate a diverse range of resources in real-time and across various timescales, transcending the artificial and ideological boundaries between named languages and between language and other semiotic systems for meaning- and sense-making. This approach requires several key methodological shifts (Li, 2022):

(1) Shift focus from language as abstract codes to emphasize meaning- and sense-making through translanguaging.
(2) Expand attention to a broader range of multi-semiotic resources, while avoiding the prioritization of specific modes or methods of meaning-making. Even subtle changes in facial expressions, body posture, or typographic choices (e.g., font size and style) can alter the meaning of a message as significantly as switching between named languages.
(3) Adopt an analytical focus on the assemblage and orchestration of diverse means of meaning- and sense-making, rather than isolating or examining one mode (linguistic or otherwise) at a time.

### 1.3.3 Capturing the Moment: Key Analytical Tools

In order to analyse the construction of translanguaging spaces and explore the creativity and criticality of multilingual practices, researchers must focus on the spontaneous and momentary performances of speakers. Moment Analysis, a methodology introduced by Li (2011), is designed to investigate these spontaneous acts of creativity and criticality in everyday social interactions. This approach centres on understanding what triggers a specific social action at a particular moment during an interaction and the consequences that follow. In this framework, the researcher examines how the use of various linguistic, multimodal, and multi-semiotic resources at a specific moment is noticed or commented on by participants, as well as what may have led to a particular action at that precise moment. In essence, Moment Analysis provides the methodological 'microscope' to examine how translanguaging spaces are constructed moment-by-moment, offering a concrete pathway for researchers to implement the theoretical principles of the framework (see Section 4.1.4 for a detailed application).

Another methodological framework for examining translanguaging at specific moments in social interaction involves the combination of Multimodal Conversation Analysis with Interpretative Phenomenological Analysis (Tai, 2023). This methodological combination enables researchers to trace how translanguaging practices emerge in multilingual classrooms and to explore how teachers interpret their own practices during particular classroom episodes. It offers a distinctive, practical toolkit for investigating multilingual interaction in linguistically and culturally diverse settings (see Section 4.2 for details).

## 1.4 Summary: Multilingual Classroom as a Translanguaging Space

Building on the discussion of translanguaging as a pedagogical practice, a theory of language, and an analytical perspective, Li (2011, 2018) introduced the concept of a 'translanguaging space' – a dynamic, interactive space created by and for translanguaging practices. Li (2011) emphasized that the construction of such a space draws on Lefebvre's (1991) spatial triad theory, which conceptualizes space as socially constructed through the interplay of perceived, conceived, and lived dimensions. According to Li (2011), the creation of a translanguaging space involves three key aspects: the cognitive, the socio-historical, and the cultural. Li (2011) described a translanguaging space not as a mere physical environment but as 'a social space for multilingual language users, integrating different dimensions of their personal history, experience, environment, attitudes, beliefs, ideologies, cognitive abilities, and physical capacities into one coordinated and meaningful performance, transforming it into a lived experience' (Li, 2011, p. 1223). This process empowers individuals to merge diverse identities, values, and practices, transcending the boundaries of syntactic structures, cognitive and semiotic systems, and modalities to create new identities, values, and practices (Li, 2011).

I argue that establishing a classroom translanguaging space can transform the learning environment into a fluid and dynamic setting where teachers and students collaboratively orchestrate multilingual, multimodal, multi-semiotic, and multi-sensory resources to co-construct meaning. A theoretical notion of translanguaging sub-space was also proposed, which argued that the division of 'translanguaging space' (Li, 2011) into different translanguaging sub-spaces can enable classroom interaction researchers to discern nuances within the broader construct and to foreground its dynamic nature (Tai, 2023). In an empirical study, Tai and Li (2025) demonstrate how multiple translanguaging sub-spaces emerge and how they allow teachers and learners to bring varied linguistic and multimodal resources and different kinds of knowledge into lessons to support understanding, meaning-making, and a range of pedagogical goals (see Section 3.1.5 for details).

This section has laid the essential theoretical groundwork, tracing the evolution of translanguaging from a pedagogical resource to a transformative theory of language and a robust analytical lens, culminating in the vision of the classroom as a translanguaging space. I have established why a translanguaging perspective is crucial for responding to multilingual realities and challenging monolingual biases.

Translanguaging as a theory of language has profound implications for the study of classroom discourse. Traditional frameworks for analysing classroom interaction, often rooted in a focus on isolated linguistic codes or a particular focus on an interactional phenomenon such as Initiation-Response-Feedback, are ill-equipped to capture the dynamic, multimodal, and multi-semiotic practices that are mobilized by multilingual teachers and students. They risk rendering invisible the very creativity, criticality, and co-construction of meaning that defines learning in these spaces. The translanguaging perspective developed in this section, therefore, is not merely an additive concept; it is a necessary recalibration of our analytical tools to properly see, hear, and understand the complex reality of multilingual classroom discourse.

The critical question that now arises is: What does this look like in practice? Having established the 'what' and the 'why', Section 2 turns to the 'how'. It will review a range of empirical studies to illustrate the concrete ways in which educators and learners across diverse global contexts actively carve out and navigate these translanguaging spaces. The review will demonstrate how, in real classrooms, participants deploy their full linguistic and semiotic repertoires to activate their funds of knowledge, thereby making meaning, deepening content learning, and fostering language development in action.

## 2 Translanguaging Practices in Multilingual Classrooms

Building directly on this imperative, Section 2 turns to the empirical heart of this Element: how translanguaging transforms the very fabric of classroom discourse. It begins by examining key interactional features of traditional classroom talk, such as the Initiation-Response-Feedback (IRF) sequence, learner initiatives, and classroom micro-contexts, to establish a baseline understanding of the structures that have long dominated classroom interaction research. It then demonstrates how a translanguaging lens fundamentally reinterprets these features, revealing how the flow of classroom discourse is enhanced when participants are enabled to engage in more fluid and dynamic exchanges using their full linguistic and semiotic repertoires.

The section will argue that translanguaging practices empower students by validating their linguistic, multimodal, and sociocultural knowledge, thereby encouraging critical thinking, creativity, and deeper understanding. Central to this argument are the notions of funds of knowledge and co-learning as pedagogical approaches that use translanguaging to facilitate inclusivity and reshape discursive power dynamics. Through a review of empirical studies from diverse settings – including EMI, EAL, online, CAL, and First Language classrooms – this section will demonstrate how translanguaging ensures effective meaning-making and enhances the quality of classroom interactions, not as a deviation from effective discourse, but as its very engine in multilingual contexts.

## 2.1 Key Interactional Features of Classroom Discourse

Classroom discourse research seeks to explore interactional features within classrooms or other educational settings. However, recent studies have expanded beyond analysing spoken language to include multimodal behaviours, as well as meso-level and macro-level policies and ideologies (e.g., Ashton, 2016). Classroom discourse has been examined from various disciplinary perspectives, including system-based approaches using coding schemes (e.g., Flanders, 1970), discourse analytic approaches (e.g., Sinclair and Coulthard, 1975; Tsui, 1985), critical discourse analytic approaches (e.g., Ashton, 2016; Weninger, 2020; Shepard-Carey, 2023), and conversation analytic approaches (e.g., Sert and Walsh, 2012; Tai and Brandt, 2018; Tam (2025); Zuo and Walsh, 2023; Zuo, 2025). Analysing classroom discourse provides valuable insights into teaching and learning processes, as the ways participants interact serve as a lens for understanding how teaching and learning are accomplished (Sert, 2015).

Previous studies on classroom interaction, particularly those centred on teacher-fronted settings, have often relied on Sinclair and Coulthard's (1975) framework for classifying classroom discourse, especially their IRF sequence. This model is characteristic of teacher-dominated classrooms and presents a fundamental conflict with the translanguaging paradigm. While translanguaging conceptualizes communication as mobile, fluid, and complex, the IRF sequence imposes a rigid, triadic structure that pre-defines participant roles and constrains the flow of discourse. While learners participate in the second phase of this sequence (the response), their contributions are primarily analysed in terms of how they reflect or influence the teacher's preceding or subsequent talk. For example, Sinclair and Coulthard (1975, p. 49) noted that the third phase (teacher feedback) is perceived as obligatory by all participants. They illustrate that when feedback is absent, other learners interpret this omission as a negative evaluation and may offer alternative responses to the teacher's initial prompt. Consequently, learner contributions are included in the coding system mainly because they relate to the categorization of teacher talk. This approach, however, tends to undervalue the potential impact of learner contributions on classroom interaction (Jacknick, 2011). The core of the problem is that the IRF model is architecturally designed to position the learner exclusively in the 'Response' slot. This structural bias renders it ill-equipped to capture the reality of student-led interaction. In authentic classroom discourse, students frequently exercise agency by initiating questions, introducing new topics, or providing unsolicited evaluations – actions that actively disrupt the predictable IRF sequence. These 'disruptions', however, are not breakdowns in communication but are vital moments of co-construction and critical thinking. By failing to accommodate them, the IRF framework presents a distorted, teacher-centric view of classroom discourse that silences the very initiatives that drive learning forward.

Several studies have criticized the IRF sequence for limiting opportunities for student participation and second language (L2) learning (Tharp and Gallimore, 1988; Nystrand, 1997). Kasper (2001, p. 518) described the IRF sequence as 'an unproductive interactional format', arguing that it serves as a tool for teacher control, leaving learners with insufficient opportunities to develop the complex interactional, linguistic, and cognitive skills needed for everyday conversation. Furthermore, coding turns for specific actions can be problematic, as a single turn by a teacher or student may serve multiple functions. Seedhouse (2004, pp. 59–62) highlighted that using a coding approach to analyse IRF cycles overlooks the fact that 'interaction is inherently dynamic, fluid, and locally managed on a turn-by-turn basis'. From a translanguaging perspective, the IRF framework is not just inadequate but antithetical, as its prescriptive structure actively suppresses the very conditions necessary for the spontaneous, multilingual, and multi-semiotic practices that characterize a translanguaging space. It cannot capture the intricate, emergent, and co-constructed nature of discourse in a multilingual classroom.

While the IRF sequence can create certain controlled learning opportunities (e.g., Seedhouse, 1994), its rigid structure is fundamentally challenged by research emphasizing learner agency as the engine of meaningful learning (e.g., Kasper, 2001; Allwright, 2005). This critique moves beyond merely expanding student talk time and instead questions the IRF's very premise: that learning is a teacher-directed, linear process. The concept of learner initiatives embodies this shift. Waring (2011, p. 204) defined learner initiatives as 'any learner attempt to make an uninvited contribution to the ongoing conversation'. Drawing on her analysis of fourteen hours of EAL classroom interactions in the US, Waring developed a typology of learner initiatives, categorizing them into three main types: (1) initiating a sequence through self-selection, (2) responding when no specific response is requested, and (3) using 'a given opportunity to do more than what is expected or the unexpected' (p. 214). Waring's study reveals that learner initiatives extend beyond simple self-selection, as learners engaged in various actions such as joking, persuading, displaying knowledge, and pursuing casual conversations. These initiatives demonstrated how learners actively accessed diverse learning opportunities by participating in classroom interactions, positioning themselves as agents of their own learning. This research is particularly valuable as it provides a foundational framework for teachers to recognize the multifaceted roles of learner initiatives in fostering classroom participation.

These learner initiatives are powerful precisely because they can reshape the trajectory of classroom discourse. Waring's (2009) study offers a compelling example, demonstrating how an EAL learner, Miyuki, strategically 'moves out' (p. 796) of a rigid IRF sequence. By interpreting the teacher's cues and seizing an opportune moment, Miyuki introduces a question about the present perfect tense, effectively derailing the teacher's planned agenda. This learner-initiated act successfully opens a dialogic space where the teacher and students collaboratively negotiate form and meaning, transforming a monologic recitation into a co-constructed exploration of language. Crucially, this reshaping of discourse is not solely a verbal accomplishment. The analysis of classroom interaction must also account for the multimodal orchestration of meaning, which often works in tandem with learner agency. In a complementary study, Tai and Brandt (2018) show how an ESOL teacher employs embodied enactments – the strategic integration of gestures, body movements, and verbal resources – to construct hypothetical scenarios for vocabulary learning. Their microanalysis reveals that comprehension is not achieved through verbal explanation alone, but through the dynamic interplay where a physical demonstration shows meaning that words alone cannot fully convey. This approach underscores that classroom discourse is a multi-semiotic flow, where verbal and non-verbal resources are inseparably fused to facilitate understanding and engagement. Together, these studies illustrate a fundamental principle: dynamic classroom discourse is co-constructed through the interplay of learner-driven initiatives and teacher-facilitated multimodal scaffolding. They demonstrate that breaking from the IRF structure is not enough; a full understanding requires an analytical lens capable of capturing how talk, gesture, and embodied action collectively create a translanguaging space where meaning is fluidly and collaboratively built.

To gain a deeper understanding of how interactions are locally managed in classrooms, Seedhouse (2004) proposed a variable perspective, illustrating that L2 classroom contexts vary, 'each with its own pedagogical focus and corresponding organization of turn-taking and sequence' (p. 101). Seedhouse (2004) contended that classroom interaction is not a uniform entity but can be categorized into several sub-varieties, including form and accuracy contexts, meaning and fluency contexts, task-oriented contexts, and procedural contexts. Each context is shaped by locally emerging and co-constructed pedagogical goals, resulting in distinct features of turn-taking, repair, and sequential organization.

In form and accuracy contexts, the primary goal is to elicit precise linguistic forms from students, requiring the teacher to maintain strict control over the turn-taking system (p. 102). In meaning and fluency contexts, the focus shifts to enabling students to communicate meaning, with minimal or no teacher interruption for explicit error correction. In task-oriented contexts, the emphasis is on task completion, which may influence the structure of the speech exchange system and turn-taking. In procedural contexts, the teacher's goal is to provide instructions before an activity begins.

Seedhouse (2004) noted that prior research on classroom interaction has often concentrated on specific action types (e.g., Markee, 1995; Morell, 2007) or particular interactional structures (e.g., Lee, 2007), portraying teachers as addressing one pedagogical goal at a time. Seedhouse challenged this view by developing a framework that highlights how L2 teachers may simultaneously orient to multiple pedagogical goals, with classroom interaction operating on multiple levels at once. This perspective underscores the complexity and dynamic nature of classroom discourse. This framework provides a vital precursor to the concept of the translanguaging sub-space (Tai and Li, 2025). Seedhouse's typology reveals the classroom not as a monolithic discursive unit, but as an ecosystem of distinct yet interconnected interactional sub-varieties. This directly informs the theoretical notion of translanguaging sub-spaces (Tai, 2023). Just as Seedhouse showed that pedagogical goals create different interactional contexts, a translanguaging perspective reveals that these same contexts afford different configurations of a student's multilingual and multimodal repertoire. Therefore, Seedhouse's demonstration of the classroom's inherent multiplicity provides the analytical groundwork for understanding how a single translanguaging space can be divided into nuanced, emergent sub-spaces. This allows researchers to move beyond a blanket observation of translanguaging to a precise analysis of how specific translanguaging sub-spaces are carved out for different pedagogical and meaning-making purposes, capturing the true complexity of multilingual classroom discourse.

## 2.2 Translanguaging as a Pedagogy for Equality and Inclusivity

The concept of translanguaging aligns with the principles of promoting equity and social justice in educational settings. This section will elaborate on this alignment through four interconnected pillars: (1) co-learning as a shift in power, (2) the integration of funds of knowledge, (3) the translanguaging stance–design–shifts framework, and (4) translanguaging as a means of decolonizing education. It emphasizes the full utilization of both teachers' and students' linguistic and multimodal repertoires. Drawing on inclusive education, culturally relevant and responsive teaching, and multicultural education frameworks (Ladson-Billings, 1995), translanguaging advocates for leveraging students' complete resources in the classroom. This approach has the potential to empower students who are often marginalized by monolingual policies in multilingual environments. Therefore, implementing inclusive practices can be seen as a process of translanguaging, where teachers actively identify and strategically utilize available resources to foster inclusive teaching in multilingual classrooms (Tai, 2022). This approach disrupts language hierarchies, enables full student participation, and supports the co-construction of new meanings and innovative language practices. In doing so, it creates a translanguaging space that facilitates meaning-making and advances social justice (Li, 2018; Hamman-Ortiz et al., 2025).

### 2.2.1 Pillar 1: Co-Learning as a Shift in Power and Mindset

To implement translanguaging as a pedagogy for inclusion and social justice, teachers must embrace a shift in mindset and discourse, distinct from traditional approaches taken by researchers and practitioners. One example of this shift is the creation of a translanguaging space for co-learning, which redefines the roles of teachers and students. As Brantmeier (2013) explained, co-learning disrupts conventional hierarchies by encouraging teachers and students to learn from one another and collaboratively construct knowledge. This approach challenges the traditional power dynamics that position the teacher as the sole authority and the students as inexperienced learners. Instead, the teacher becomes 'a learning facilitator', 'a scaffolder', and 'a critical reflection enhancer', while students take on roles as 'empowered explorers', 'meaning makers', and 'responsible knowledge constructors' (Brantmeier, 2013, p. 97).

Co-learning also rejects the privileging of one form of knowledge over another (Curry and Cunningham, 2000; Tai and Li, 2021a), emphasizing that all knowledge – acquired through diverse languages and cultural contexts – holds equal value. In an inclusive classroom, co-learning fosters mutual respect among knowledge sharers and cultivates a sense of care and collaboration among participants. Brantmeier (2013) connected co-learning to his concept of a pedagogy of vulnerability, which relieves teachers of the pressure to have all the answers and encourages them to take risks – 'risks of self-disclosure, risks of change, risks of not knowing, risks of failing' – to deepen the learning experience (p. 96). In essence, co-learning involves acknowledging that no one, including the teacher, knows everything.

While translanguaging emphasizes the respect for all languages and promotes learning through diverse linguistic and cultural perspectives, co-learning extends this respect to the knowledge, values, and insights of all participants. Both concepts advocate for creating opportunities for varied ways of learning and discussing learning, as well as dismantling asymmetrical power relationships in educational settings. Together, both notions highlight the importance of fostering equitable and inclusive learning environments. This culture of co-learning establishes the necessary classroom ethos for the next critical pillar: the integration of students' funds of knowledge. When teachers reposition themselves as co-learners, they create the relational safety and mutual respect required for students to confidently share the culturally developed knowledge from their homes and communities.

### 2.2.2 Pillar 2: Integrating Funds of Knowledge

As I mentioned earlier, teaching for equity and social justice not only incorporates students' diverse linguistic and multimodal resources into learning opportunities but also builds on their funds of knowledge (García and Li, 2014). These funds of knowledge are defined as 'the historically accumulated and culturally developed bodies of knowledge and skills essential for household and individual functioning and well-being' (Moll et al., 1992, p. 133). Research by Moll et al. (1992) highlights that when teachers step away from their traditional roles as experts and instead position themselves as collaborative learners, they gain a deeper and more nuanced understanding of students' lived experiences and the knowledge they bring from their families and communities. By leveraging these diverse funds of knowledge, teachers can transform classroom interactions, moving beyond repetitive, memorization-based instruction to create more dynamic and meaningful learning experiences. This approach benefits both teachers and students, fostering a collaborative learning environment that promotes inclusivity, meaning-making, and identity exploration – elements often neglected in traditional education (Li, 2014; Tai, 2025d). Thus, establishing a translanguaging space that integrates diverse funds of knowledge and encourages co-learning allows multilingual students to feel valued and respected for who they are. It acknowledges their lived experiences, identities, language use, and their capacity for creativity and critical thinking, creating a more inclusive and empowering educational environment.

Integrating these funds of knowledge, however, cannot be a sporadic activity; it requires a pedagogical framework. This is where the translanguaging stance–design–shifts model becomes essential, providing a tool for guiding teachers' development of translanguaging pedagogies and responsively adapting to the diverse knowledge students bring into the classroom discourse.

### 2.2.3 Pillar 3: Translanguaging Stance-Design-Shifts Framework

A pivotal framework for enacting translanguaging as pedagogy – the pedagogical philosophy that empowers learners by leveraging their full linguistic and semiotic repertoires – is the widely cited model of translanguaging stance, design, and shifts (García et al., 2017). This framework provides a structure for teachers to implement the guiding principle of translanguaging as pedagogy in their practice. Crucially, this framework must be distinguished from pedagogical translanguaging (Cenoz and Gorter, 2021), which refers to specific, planned instructional practices that utilize two or more languages. While pedagogical translanguaging is a descriptive label for a set of techniques, the stance–design–shifts framework embodies the broader, transformative philosophy of translanguaging pedagogy. The framework is defined by three interdependent components:

(1) A translanguaging stance is the 'firm belief that their students' language practices are both a resource and a right' and that 'the many different language practices of bilingual students work juntos/together' (García et al., 2017, p. 27).
(2) Translanguaging design involves the strategic planning of curricula, instruction, and assessment to intentionally incorporate and value students' full semiotic repertoires.
(3) Translanguaging shifts are the unplanned, moment-to-moment adjustments teachers make to respond to students' emergent learning needs and feedback.

When applied, this framework guides teachers to affirm multilingual students' diverse knowledge systems rather than demand conformity to a monolingual norm. Simply implementing isolated multilingual activities, or pedagogical translanguaging, is insufficient. For these strategies to be genuinely effective and culturally responsive, they must be rooted in the deeper philosophical commitment of translanguaging pedagogy. This means a teacher's practice must be guided by an authentic stance that values students' full linguistic repertoires as a right and resource, a design that intentionally integrates these repertoires into learning, and the flexibility to make in-the-moment shifts.

Without this foundational philosophy, multilingual strategies risk becoming just another procedural method that fails to challenge the monolingual biases and power structures translanguaging seeks to dismantle. In essence, the framework ensures that the how (pedagogical translanguaging) is always guided by the why (translanguaging pedagogy), serving as the essential bridge between its transformative principle and concrete, context-sensitive classroom interaction.

Ultimately, the stance–design–shifts framework is more than a pedagogical tool; it is a mechanism for decolonization. The *stance* directly challenges raciolinguistic ideologies, the *design* deliberately centres marginalized knowledge systems, and the *shifts* continuously cede epistemic authority to students, thereby actively erasing the 'abyssal line' in classroom discourse.

### 2.2.4 Pillar 4: Translanguaging as a Means of Decolonizing Education

Beyond its role in challenging linguistic and modal boundaries, translanguaging functions as a decisive decolonial project. It actively works to restore the knowledge systems and cultural-linguistic practices that colonization systematically erased, thereby creating avenues for social and cognitive justice in education (García et al., 2021; Li and García, 2022; Rajendram et al., 2023; Tian and Rafi, 2023). Central to this project is a direct confrontation with the ideology of 'academic language'. Rather than a neutral descriptor, this concept is a mechanism that privileges the language practices of dominant groups while systematically dismissing the creative, critical, and inherently academic capacities of minoritized bilinguals (Li, 2011; Flores, 2020). This raises a pivotal question: can the dynamic translanguaging of bilingual students ever be recognized as genuinely 'academic'?

The failure to do so stems from what decolonial scholar Boaventura de Sousa Santos (2014) calls the 'abyssal line' – a colonial divide that reserves epistemic power for those with dominant linguistic and racial profiles. To cross this line, educators must dismantle raciolinguistic ideologies that automatically frame racialized students as linguistically deficient (Flores, 2020). Adopting a perspective from the 'other side of the line' allows teachers to perceive the academic brilliance within students' multilingual performances. In this decolonial initiative, translanguaging pedagogy seeks to erase the abyssal line by fostering an ecology of knowledges (Heugh, 2021). This is a call for educators to critically examine their own assumptions and recognize that students' cultural and linguistic backgrounds are not deficits to overcome, but essential, valuable resources that are fundamental to academic achievement and transformative learning.

This theoretical imperative for a systemic shift is powerfully illustrated in practice. A recent study of Global South graduate students in Canada by Rajendram et al. (2023) affirms that translanguaging is vital for their knowledge acquisition and identity affirmation. Crucially, however, their research demonstrates that implementing translanguaging as a top-down, tokenistic strategy merely reinforces the very linguistic hierarchies a decolonial project seeks to dismantle. For translanguaging to function as a genuine decolonizing force, it must catalyse the systemic transformation called for above: it must be treated as a fundamental right, not a concession, which necessitates diversifying faculty, embedding it into curriculum and assessment, and comprehensively training educators. Ultimately, the study confirms that erasing the abyssal line requires centring the knowledge and linguistic practices of the Global South as inherently valuable and legitimate within the academy, thereby reconfiguring its very power dynamics.

These four pillars are not isolated strategies but are deeply interdependent, forming the foundational structure of a transformative translanguaging pedagogy. They operate synergistically: a translanguaging stance (Pillar 3) is the mindset that makes co-learning (Pillar 1) possible, which in turn is the relational approach needed to authentically uncover and integrate students' funds of knowledge (Pillar 2). Collectively, this triad of stance, relationship, and content constitutes the practical enactment of translanguaging as a decolonizing project (Pillar 4), working to dismantle oppressive hierarchies and create truly equitable learning spaces.

In the subsequent sections, I will examine empirical research that highlights the characteristics of teachers' translanguaging practices across various classroom contexts in order to support students' content and language learning and create an inclusive learning environment for all multilingual students. The studies reviewed in the subsequent sections investigate translanguaging in classroom interactions, with all authors utilizing interactional data. Some studies also incorporate interview and/or questionnaire data to triangulate findings with classroom discourse analysis, providing a more comprehensive understanding of translanguaging practices.

## 2.3 Reviewing Translanguaging in Different Classroom Contexts

### 2.3.1 English-Medium-Instruction and Content and Language Integrated Learning Classrooms

CLIL is defined as 'an educational approach that utilizes various language-supportive methodologies to deliver dual-focused instruction, emphasizing both language and content' (Coyle et al., 2010, p. 3). The primary goal of

CLIL is to teach an L2 alongside subject-specific content, enabling students to enhance their L2 proficiency while gaining knowledge in academic disciplines. CLIL programs provide flexibility in selecting the language of instruction, although English is commonly used (Macaro, 2018). In contrast, EMI has been defined in various ways, but Macaro (2018) provided a concise definition that captures its core characteristics. He describes EMI as 'the use of the English language to teach academic subjects (other than English itself) in countries or regions where the majority of the population does not speak English as their first language' (p. 19). Unlike CLIL, EMI is positioned within the content-oriented domain, as its primary focus is on content learning, with L2 English acquisition being a secondary outcome. In EMI programs, students are assessed on their content knowledge in English (L2), rather than their English language proficiency. Therefore, it can be argued that EMI differs from CLIL in its objectives and focus. While CLIL maintains a dual emphasis on both language and content – even if the balance is skewed, such as 90 per cent content and 10 per cent language – EMI prioritizes content delivery, with language learning occurring incidentally rather than intentionally. This distinction highlights the varying pedagogical approaches and goals of these two educational models.

Hence, in this section, I will differentiate between research on translanguaging in EMI and CLIL contexts. By doing so, I aim to highlight the distinct research settings, how authors conceptualize translanguaging in their studies, the target participants, and the methodological designs employed. This distinction will provide a clearer understanding of the unique contributions and implications of translanguaging research across these two educational models.

The role of translanguaging has been extensively explored in both EMI and CLIL classroom contexts (e.g., Li and Lin, 2019; Lu et al., 2023; Tai and Li, 2023; Zhu and Wang, 2024; Ruiz de Zarobe and Querol-Julián, 2025). A recent systematic review by Lu et al. (2023) analysed 103 empirical studies published between April 2015 and May 2022, identifying five major research themes in the field: (1) translanguaging practices in pedagogy, (2) translanguaging practices and language ideologies, (3) translanguaging practices in teacher-student and peer interactions, and (4) the impact of translanguaging on content and language learning. The first theme, translanguaging practices in pedagogy, examines the forms and functions of translanguaging in classroom settings. Studies under the second theme, translanguaging practices and language ideologies, reveal that teachers generally hold positive attitudes towards translanguaging, believing it enhances teaching and learning while boosting students' self-confidence. Classroom-based research further supports the positive effects of translanguaging on both language and content learning. A recent bibliometric analysis by Zhu and Wang (2024) highlighted translanguaging as a promising and critical area for developing multilingualism in EMI contexts. The analysis also identifies scholars such as Kevin W. H. Tai, Li Wei, Pramod Sah, and Prem Phyak as prolific contributors to advancing research on translanguaging in EMI classroom contexts.

Building on these insights, the following sections will explore specific empirical studies on translanguaging in EMI and CLIL classroom interactions, highlighting their unique contributions to understanding how translanguaging practices shape students' content and language learning.

### EMI Classroom Contexts

Research on translanguaging in EMI contexts has examined how teachers and students mobilize multilingual and multimodal resources to support the learning of abstract content knowledge (e.g., Lin and He, 2017; Paulsrud et al., 2021; Tai and Li, 2021b; Zhou et al., 2021; Ou and Gu, 2022; Sah and Li, 2022; Bozbiyik and Morton, 2025; Gu et al., 2023; Tai and Li, 2023; Zheng and Qiu, 2024). Lin and He (2017) conducted an ethnographic study to explore how translanguaging serves as a pedagogical strategy for an EMI science teacher to engage South Asian ethnic minority students from Pakistan, Nepal, and India, encouraging them to draw on their multilingual repertoires. The study involved ethnographic observations of classroom interactions in a year 9 EMI science classroom in Hong Kong, alongside interviews to gain insights into the students' use of Urdu phrases during lessons. The findings reveal that students utilized both their home language (Urdu) and English, along with gestures and body language, to demonstrate their understanding of the human digestive system. Notably, the teacher leveraged her prior knowledge of Urdu, acquired from her students, to provide instructions in the learners' L1. The study highlights that despite the teacher and students coming from different linguistic and cultural backgrounds, their mutual willingness to learn from each other's linguistic and cultural resources created a collaborative learning space. This environment motivated students to engage with the subject content in their L2 while expanding their linguistic repertoires for communication. This research contributes to the conceptualization of translanguaging as pedagogy, demonstrating how the full multilingual and multimodal repertoires of both teachers and students can be harnessed to develop new understandings and co-construct knowledge. It underscores the transformative potential of translanguaging in fostering inclusive and effective learning environments in EMI contexts.

Tai's research (e.g., Tai and Li, 2020, 2021a, 2021b, 2023; Tai, 2022, 2025a) has significantly deepened our understanding of translanguaging as pedagogy by conducting detailed analyses of classroom interactions to uncover the complexities of translanguaging practices in EMI contexts. Using Multimodal Conversation Analysis and Interpretative Phenomenological Analysis, Tai and Li (2021b) revealed that translanguaging serves as a critical resource for constructing playful talk, enabling an EMI mathematics teacher to achieve pedagogical goals. The sequential analysis of interactions demonstrates that playful talk facilitates content learning and fosters meaningful communication between teachers and students. This study highlights how translanguaging can act as a source of creativity and language play, allowing participants to integrate a variety of linguistic resources (e.g., smiley voice, laughter, tone, word choice), multimodal resources (e.g., gestures, drawings), pedagogical knowledge, personal experiences, and interests into lessons. In doing so, translanguaging challenges the misconception that English should dominate as the sole norm in EMI classrooms.

Similarly, Tai (2024b) explored how creating a translanguaging space provides opportunities for an EMI teacher to connect content-related knowledge, supporting students' learning of new material in an EMI Western History classroom. The findings reveal that the teacher's translanguaging practices rely heavily on diverse gestural and visual resources. These resources enable the teacher to incorporate students' Cantonese contributions and reframe them using more pedagogically relevant terminology in the target L2 (English). Theoretically, this study demonstrates that EMI classrooms can transform into translanguaging spaces where teachers and students engage in multiple meaning-making systems. These spaces allow participants to draw on knowledge from other content subjects to scaffold the teaching and learning of new material. Such translanguaging spaces not only promote fluid language practices but also encourage the integration of multiple epistemologies, helping students grasp new academic knowledge within novel interactional contexts.

Zhou et al. (2021) carried out a mixed-method study in an EMI finance classroom at an international school in China to explore students' translanguaging practices during classroom interactions and their attitudes towards using translanguaging as a teaching strategy. Through content analysis of classroom interactions and semi-structured interviews, the findings indicate that students engage in translanguaging primarily for ease of communication, supported by contextual resources and their strategic use of linguistic abilities. While students generally view translanguaging positively as a tool for enhancing content learning in EMI settings, some expressed concerns about its acceptance, noting that it might reduce exposure to English, potentially hindering their performance in EMI classes. This finding aligns with Allard's (2017) assertion that while translanguaging aids communication between teachers and students and improves access to content, it may not be seen as a transformative teaching practice due to monolingual language ideologies among students and the lack of a multilingual language policy at the school. Consequently, the authors recommended that EMI teachers should be cautious about oversimplifying translanguaging as a teaching method. They advised teachers to fully understand students' perspectives on translanguaging as a pedagogical approach to better tailor their linguistic choices in the classroom. Despite its contribution, this study conceptualizes translanguaging narrowly as switching between named languages, which indicates that translanguaging is not understood as a process of creating meanings through using multilingual and multimodal resources.

Gu et al. (2023) analysed semi-structured interviews with nine students from various disciplines, along with observations from EMI classes at different Chinese universities, to examine their learning experiences in EMI settings, the challenges they face, and their use of translanguaging by leveraging diverse multilingual and multimodal resources to enhance their understanding. The results indicate that EMI teachers actively seek effective practices for EMI programs, displaying language awareness in content teaching. Their approach is neither strictly monolingual nor monocultural; rather, it incorporates both their own and their students' linguistic and semiotic resources. The authors suggested that the medium-of-instruction should be seen not merely as a language policy, but as a process involving translanguaging to better convey complex ideas to students. However, the study did not perform a detailed analysis of classroom interactions, relying largely on interviews and photographs to demonstrate how EMI teachers effectively use semiotic and spatial resources to support teaching and learning in EMI contexts. Hence, the analysis overlooks some nuances of the classroom dynamics and the real-time application of translanguaging strategies in the EMI classrooms.

## CLIL Classroom Contexts

Research on translanguaging in CLIL contexts has primarily focused on how translanguaging supports students' content and L2 learning (e.g., Jakonen et al., 2018; Nikula and Moore, 2019; Wu and Lin, 2019; Rafi and Morgan, 2023; Nikula et al., 2025; Wong and Tian, 2025). Nikula and Moore (2019) conducted an exploratory study examining translanguaging in various secondary CLIL classrooms, including biology in Finland, technology in Spain, and history in Austria. Using qualitative discourse analysis, the authors analysed classroom interactions and found that both teachers and students employed translanguaging practices to achieve various communicative goals, such as engaging in language play, addressing pedagogical and interpersonal concerns, and delivering classroom instructions. It is important to note that the analysis in this study focuses exclusively on linguistic practices, conceptualizing translanguaging as the switching between named languages in classroom settings. This narrow perspective overlooks the role of multimodality as part of the broader repertoire for facilitating meaning-making. Moreover, the study's discourse analysis of classroom talk is relatively simplistic and brief compared to more detailed analyses, such as those by Wu and Lin (2019) and Tai and Li (2020, 2021b). These studies employ fine-grained analyses of classroom interactions to uncover the specific functions of translanguaging in EMI settings, offering deeper insights into its pedagogical and interactional roles.

Wong and Tian's (2025) study highlights the effectiveness of teacher-researcher collaboration in enabling CLIL teachers to adopt a translanguaging stance, implement translanguaging designs, and make translanguaging shifts. In their research, they employed a participatory approach to co-design lessons with two CLIL teachers in a Chinese immersion program. The authors focused on pedagogical translanguaging during the co-design process and investigated its application to support students' content and language learning in a unit on Democracy. Using a methodological framework that combines Multimodal Conversation Analysis with ethnographic methods, the findings reveal that collaboration with the CLIL teachers helped alleviate their concerns about using English, demonstrated the advantages of translanguaging pedagogies, and improved their ability to flexibly integrate the researchers' suggestions into their teaching practices. The study also notes that the teachers' use of multimodal and multilingual resources, along with their lived experiences, provided students with multiple pathways to grasp the complex concept of democracy. Furthermore, the research underscores the importance of teachers and school leaders being open-minded and genuinely willing to learn and experiment with translanguaging strategies. This openness is crucial for fostering an inclusive and effective learning environment that leverages students' full linguistic and cultural repertoires.

Rafi and Morgan (2023) investigated the role of translanguaging in Bangladeshi CLIL anthropology classrooms. The study employed a two-step ethnographic research design: first, a linguistic ethnography of undergraduate anthropology classes was conducted, followed by an auto-ethnography documenting a pedagogical intervention using translanguaging approaches. While the intervention involved both students and the lecturer, the lecturer rejected the use of translanguaging as a pedagogical resource. The findings, analysed through thematic coding, revealed that the teacher used translanguaging to deliver oral and written instructions, and students translanguaged in response. However, despite the course content including scholarly works in English, Bangla, and a mix of both, the lecturer did not strategically leverage these resources to support students' content learning. For instance, the lecturer avoided providing L1 translations of abstract academic vocabulary, instead instructing students to use a dictionary. Additionally, students translanguaged spontaneously, mirroring everyday bilingual practices, without demonstrating intentional efforts to develop L2 English proficiency or maintain academic Bangla skills. The authors argue that the lack of pedagogically informed translanguaging practices hindered students' comprehension of complex materials and their development of subject-specific language proficiency. This resulted in a teacher-centred, didactic teaching style with limited student engagement. However, a significant limitation of the study is its reliance on researchers' field notes from classroom observations, as no audio or video recordings were collected. This absence of recorded data prevented a fine-grained analysis of how translanguaging practices supported or constrained students' content and language learning, limiting the depth of the study's insights.

### 2.3.2 English as an Additional Language Classrooms

In recent years, a growing body of literature has explored how translanguaging spaces can be created in EAL classrooms to support students' L2 English learning and acquisition (e.g., Ollerhead, 2019; Galante, 2020; Mendoza, 2022; Zuo and Walsh, 2023; Lin and Leung, 2024; Tai, 2024f; Tai and Dai, 2024). In this section, I use the term 'EAL' as an inclusive and neutral term that does not specify ethnic background or assume a particular sequence of language acquisition. Similar to EMI contexts, EAL classrooms often adhere to a monolingual English-only policy, where teachers and students are expected to use English exclusively for teaching and learning. Institutions promoting the benefits of learning EAL often justify this choice by emphasizing English's role as a global language, highlighting advantages such as improved employment prospects, financial opportunities, and enhanced social and global mobility (Li, 2021; Tian and Li, 2024). The studies reviewed in this section emphasize that translanguaging plays a crucial role in validating the linguistic and cultural knowledge that EAL learners already possess. This knowledge is valuable in its own right and must be recognized as an essential component of ensuring these learners' educational success. By advocating for translanguaging, these studies highlight the importance of leveraging students' existing linguistic and cultural resources to create more inclusive and effective learning environments.

Zuo and Walsh's (2023) study utilizes Conversation Analysis to explore how EAL university teachers employ translation to construct meaning during classroom interactions. The analysis, framed from a translanguaging perspective, reveals how teachers leverage both linguistic and paralinguistic resources across different modes – managerial, materials, and classroom context – to facilitate understanding and carry out actions through translation. In the managerial mode, teachers use translation to address interactional breakdowns, provide task instructions by supplementing textbook directions with L1 explanations, and translate challenging vocabulary into students' L1. The authors argue that translation is not a static practice, as the analysis demonstrates teachers' dynamic use of linguistic and paralinguistic resources across various modes. This aligns with the concept of translanguaging, where EAL teachers adapt their language use based on the interactional context and immediate pedagogical goals. However, it is worth noting that while the authors recognize translanguaging as a process of mobilizing a multilingual's full repertoire, their analysis focuses solely on linguistic and paralinguistic features. The study does not capture the use of multimodal resources (e.g., gestures, visuals) in the translation process during EAL classroom interactions, leaving room for further exploration of how broader semiotic resources contribute to meaning-making in multilingual classrooms.

Drawing on the perspective of translanguaging as a theory of language, which emphasizes mobilizing multilinguals' full linguistic, multimodal resources, and diverse funds of knowledge, Ollerhead (2019) explored how an EAL teacher implemented translanguaging pedagogical approaches with culturally and linguistically diverse migrant students at an intensive English centre in Australia. The study collected multiple data sources, including lesson recordings, co-planning sessions with the teacher, and stimulated-recall interviews. Thematic and qualitative analyses of classroom interactions were used to examine the data. The findings reveal that, despite identifying as monolingual, the teacher adopted a multilingual stance through her translanguaging strategies. Her carefully designed, collaborative learning approach, rooted in translanguaging, enabled students to strategically use diverse linguistic and semiotic resources, enriching their learning experiences. The study highlights three key positive outcomes for students: (1) expanded vocabularies and increased metalinguistic and meta-semantic awareness; (2) richer, more sensory, and embodied literacy learning experiences; and (3) enhanced literacy engagement through the recognition and celebration of students' linguistic and cultural funds of knowledge. These outcomes underscore the transformative potential of translanguaging in fostering inclusive and effective learning environments for multilingual students.

Similarly, Lin and Leung (2024) conducted a detailed Conversation Analysis, enhanced by a multimodal transcription system, to study EAL classroom interactions among Taiwanese L1 Mandarin students at a UK university. The study aimed to explore the benefits of creating a translanguaging space for advancing classroom instruction. The analysis reveals that both the teacher and students leverage linguistic and non-linguistic resources to make sense of the learning content and collaboratively construct knowledge in real-time. The authors argue that establishing a translanguaging space supports the scaffolding of instructions and enhances comprehension, ultimately achieving the pedagogical goal of improving students' understanding of phrasal verbs and multi-word constructions. Additionally, the study highlights that translanguaging encourages and empowers all participants – students and teachers alike – to share their knowledge and experiences, co-construct knowledge, and even challenge traditional classroom authority. This process fosters an environment where linguistic diversity is embraced and valued, promoting a more inclusive and dynamic learning experience.

### 2.3.3 Online Language Classrooms

The COVID-19 pandemic has accelerated the adoption of synchronous online teaching for delivering real-time L2 learning lessons. This shift to online platforms has significantly transformed formal learning environments, offering flexibility that traditional face-to-face teaching often cannot provide (Moorhouse et al., 2022). However, teaching through synchronous online platforms presents unique challenges, particularly in how teachers can effectively communicate with students to facilitate language learning. Recent studies have explored how translanguaging can be utilized in online language classrooms to mediate students' L2 learning and enhance engagement in virtual settings (e.g., Atar and Rafi, 2024; Tai, 2024c; Tai, 2025d; Tai and Zuo, 2024). These studies highlight the potential of translanguaging to create more inclusive and interactive online learning experiences, addressing the complexities of virtual communication and fostering student participation.

Atar and Rafi (2024) used Conversation Analysis as their methodological framework to examine how translanguaging practices are manifested in EAL online classrooms at a Turkish university. The authors suggest that their findings highlight how translanguaging pedagogy can support the creative, critical, and strategic use of bilingual students' full linguistic repertoires in classroom practices. However, the actual analysis primarily reveals significant inefficiencies, such as wasted time during classroom interactions, with the authors later applying a translanguaging pedagogy lens to interpret these practices. For instance, the teacher's repeated attempts to address misunderstandings – through strategies like rephrasing, repetition, nominating individual students, and serial nominations – are framed as translanguaging pedagogies. Hence, it can be argued that the authors' understanding of translanguaging is limited to the use of paralinguistic and interactional resources, rather than encompassing the broader mobilization of multilingual and multimodal resources by classroom participants to scaffold students' EAL learning. This narrow interpretation overlooks the full potential of translanguaging as a pedagogical approach that integrates diverse linguistic, cultural, and semiotic resources to create more inclusive and effective learning environments.

Tai (2025) expanded on existing research exploring how translanguaging serves as a resource to integrate diverse funds of knowledge into classrooms, enhancing students' content and language learning. The study investigates how an EAL teacher interactionally conveys sociocultural values and beliefs – such as attitudes and beliefs related to race, ethnicity, and diversity – through translanguaging to enrich students' EAL learning experiences. Using Multimodal Conversation Analysis and Interpretative Phenomenological Analysis, the study analyses online classroom interactions and video-stimulated recall interviews. The findings reveal that the EAL teacher effectively leverages various funds of knowledge and screen-based multimodal resources to foster specific sociocultural values and beliefs. For instance, the teacher incorporates historical facts, personal stories, and life experiences into online English lessons. Translanguaging emerges as a crucial resource for facilitating the communication of sociocultural values and beliefs to students. The study conceptualizes the online language classroom as a virtual translanguaging space, where teachers and students bring diverse funds of knowledge into the learning process. This space bridges the gap between L2 learning and everyday life experiences, promoting not only facts and practices but also values and ideologies. The study underscores the importance of moving beyond rote learning and knowledge acquisition in EAL teaching. Instead, teachers should foster students' critical thinking, creativity, and positive values and attitudes – such as open-mindedness – to equip them with the skills and knowledge needed to navigate today's society. This approach highlights the transformative potential of translanguaging in creating meaningful and inclusive learning experiences.

Drawing on the same methodological approach, Tai (2024c) explored how online EAL teachers create a translanguaging space by adapting resources from face-to-face classroom contexts to online environments to support students' EAL learning. The findings reveal that the multimodal resources commonly used in traditional classroom settings transcend the boundaries of mode in a social semiotic sense, as they are re-enacted in online tutorials to enhance the process of virtual teaching. For instance, the teacher's reliance on an online dictionary serves as a resource for teaching new vocabulary, consistently utilized in both traditional and online teaching environments. These findings challenge the artificial divides between linguistic and non-linguistic dimensions of language teaching, as well as the ideological separation between face-to-face and online settings. Building on this analysis, the study introduces the concept of 'multimodal language instruction' as a new perspective, replacing the traditional view of instruction as confined to physical settings, time, and facilities. Theoretically, this notion emphasizes that L2 instruction is inherently mobile and multimodal, not limited to formal, physical environments but also occurring in informal and online spaces where learning unfolds.

### 2.3.4 Chinese as an Additional Language Classrooms

An increasing number of students globally are learning CAL, mostly after learning English or one or two other important languages in their home countries (Lo Bianco, 2007; Wang, 2014). Their arrival has resulted in linguistically diverse classrooms, posing a huge challenge to the monolingual teaching approach that prevails in most CAK classrooms in and outside China. Innovative pedagogies to make Chinese teaching more accessible to multilingual students have become a pressing research agenda for CAL teaching professionals to achieve effective learning outcomes in many countries and regions (e.g., Bao and Du, 2015; Zhang et al., 2015). Due to the fast-growing scholarly interests in Chinese as a global language, there is a considerable number of studies examining the affordances of creating a translanguaging space in CAL classrooms to validate students' multilingual and multimodal repertoires and promote CAL learning opportunities (e.g., Li, 2014; Wang, 2019, 2023; Tai and Lee, 2024).

Wang (2019) investigated students' and teachers' perceptions and practices regarding translanguaging in beginner-level CAL university classrooms. The study employed a mixed-methods approach, including a questionnaire survey to gauge students' attitudes, in-depth interviews to explore teachers' perspectives, and classroom observations to analyse language practices in natural settings. Discourse analysis of the CAL classroom interactions revealed that translanguaging practices, initiated by both teachers and students, empowered students to negotiate meaning, validated their contributions, and fostered rapport among all participants. This study highlights the role of translanguaging in creating inclusive and collaborative learning environments.

Building on her earlier work, Wang (2023) explored how Chinese language teachers in Hong Kong used translanguaging as a social justice strategy to address challenges in teaching ethnic minority students, particularly South Asians (e.g., Indians, Nepalese, Pakistanis, Sri Lankans), in a monolingual educational setting. Using thematic analysis, Wang categorized the pedagogical functions of translanguaging in classroom discourse and collected teacher interviews to understand their perceptions and rationales for adopting such strategies. The analysis revealed that teachers adopted a translanguaging stance, leveraging L2 English and Cantonese to create more inclusive and equitable learning environments for ethnic minority students. Interviews further highlighted teachers' growing awareness of classroom diversity and broader social inequalities, including racial discrimination.

However, Wang's (2023) study lacks evidence of how teachers incorporated students' home languages (e.g., Urdu, Punjabi) into classroom interactions, as the analysed examples only involved switching between English and Cantonese. This raises concerns about students' ability to fully grasp Chinese syntax and vocabulary explanations using only L2 English, potentially hindering their CAL learning. This aligns with Sah and Li's (2022) and Tai's (2025b) concept of 'unequal translanguaging', where certain linguistic or multimodal resources are prioritized over others. In this case, the overreliance on English and Cantonese, at the expense of students' home languages, reflects unequal translanguaging. Additionally, like Atar and Rafi (2024) and Zuo and Walsh (2023), Wang's studies (2019, 2023) narrowly conceptualize translanguaging as switching between named languages, rather than viewing it as multilinguals' ability to make meaning through diverse linguistic and semiotic resources. This limited perspective overlooks the full potential of translanguaging in fostering inclusive and equitable learning environments.

Using interactional sociolinguistics, Li (2014) examined classroom interactions between teachers and students in a UK Chinese heritage language classroom. The study highlights how classroom participants freely switch between different varieties of Chinese, English, and various modes of communication. Li also emphasizes that students bring not only their multilingual skills but also their knowledge of the social world – such as their awareness of their community's history, their positions within it, and their personal attitudes and beliefs – into the learning process. Li argued that students' creative and critical expressions in their schoolwork reflect their agency in shaping their sociocultural identities, attitudes, and values, challenging the dominance of Mandarin as the Chinese lingua franca. These translanguaging practices extend beyond pedagogy and learning, potentially influencing students' identity development, social relationships, and value systems. This underscores the broader sociocultural impact of translanguaging in heritage language education.

Recent research by Tian and Lau (2022, 2023) provides detailed insights into how translanguaging spaces are collaboratively constructed in Mandarin immersion programs in the US. Their work highlights how students who primarily speak English participate in critical sociolinguistic exploration and build multilingual identities through CAL learning. In their 2022 study, Tian and Lau conducted an in-depth examination of Chinese teaching methods and carried out a multimodal analysis of third graders' Chinese character artwork as a form of visual storytelling. Classroom observations revealed that both teachers and students drew on a variety of linguistic and semiotic resources to make meaning together – such as switching between Chinese and Pinyin scripts, blending English and Mandarin, and using visual imagery and gestures to create stories and depict the target character '田' (field). The authors argue that the teacher's strategic use of these resources helps students deepen their understanding of the Chinese language, especially in terms of radicals, pictographic origins, and visual approaches to interpreting Chinese characters.

### 2.3.5 English as a First Language Classrooms

I conclude Section 2 by reviewing translanguaging studies in the context of English as an L1 classroom. While current research has extensively explored how teachers implement pedagogical translanguaging in multilingual settings and its impact on students' content and language learning (e.g., Lin and He, 2017; Sah and Li, 2022; Zuo and Walsh, 2023; Lin and Leung, 2024), few studies have examined how teachers trained in translanguaging apply this pedagogy in L1 English classrooms.

Existing research highlights that many L1 English classrooms in the US enforce restrictive language policies that marginalize students whose language practices deviate from 'standard English' (de los Ríos and Seltzer, 2017; Seltzer, 2019). However, these studies often rely on students' and teachers' metacommentaries about their practices, lacking a fine-grained analysis of classroom discourse. This gap limits researchers' and educators' understanding of how integrating students' diverse linguistic and multimodal practices can challenge monolingual ideologies. To date, studies demonstrating how teachers create translanguaging spaces in L1 settings remain scarce. Investigating translanguaging practices in L1 English classrooms is crucial, as it can offer new insights into how teachers leverage multilingual and multimodal resources to expand native English students' communicative repertoires and foster appreciation for linguistic and cultural diversity in today's society.

Tai and Wong's (2023) study addresses a gap in Applied Linguistics by providing a fine-grained analysis of how teachers use translanguaging as a pedagogical resource to facilitate meaning-making and knowledge construction in an L1 English classroom composed solely of native English-speaking students. Using Multimodal Conversation Analysis, the findings illustrate how Miss T, the native English teacher, expands students' linguistic repertoires by teaching Spanish words, connecting this learning to students' lived experiences, and co-creating imaginary scenarios through diverse multilingual and multimodal resources. The Interpretative Phenomenological Analysis of Miss T's stimulated-recall interview reveals her pedagogical goals of integrating L2 Spanish words into the L1 English classroom. The interview underscores her dedication to expanding students' linguistic knowledge, fostering equal learning opportunities and social inclusion, and, crucially, cultivating students as humble learners who are open to learning from others. Hence, this study indicates Miss T's initiative to create a translanguaging space in an L1 English classroom, demonstrating its transformative impact on students' learning. Such a space reshapes students' perceptions of languages as communicative resources and encourages appreciation for linguistic and cultural diversity within their community. The study argues that the need to enhance communicative repertoires extends beyond multilingual learners; even native L1 speakers must develop the ability to strategically use available resources and knowledge to achieve specific communicative goals in social interactions. This perspective challenges traditional notions of language learning and highlights the universal value of translanguaging in fostering inclusive and dynamic educational environments.

## 2.4 Summary

Building on the theoretical foundations of Section 1, this section presents the empirical case for how translanguaging transforms classroom discourse, arguing that it serves as the essential engine for effective communication in multilingual settings rather than a deviation from it. The section establishes this by first critiquing the limitations of traditional, rigid interaction models like the IRF sequence, which suppresses learner agency and multimodal meaning-making, and then showcasing how translanguaging practices – through learner initiatives, multimodal orchestration, and the creation of nuanced translanguaging sub-spaces – empower students by leveraging their full linguistic and semiotic repertoires. Framed as a pedagogy for equity, translanguaging is operationalized through co-learning, which reshapes power dynamics, and the integration of students' funds of knowledge, a point substantiated by a review of empirical studies across diverse contexts (EMI, CLIL, EAL, Online, CAL, and L1 English classrooms) that collectively demonstrate how this approach fosters inclusive, co-constructed learning environments that enhance meaning-making, content understanding, and identity affirmation.

## 3 Expanding the Conceptualization of Translanguaging: Theoretical Development and Implications for Pedagogy

### 3.1 Development of New Theoretical Notions

In the field of Applied Linguistics, researchers have been using translanguaging as an analytical perspective to rethink existing theoretical concepts, enhancing our comprehension of the complexities involved in interactional phenomena. This section aims to elucidate how the concept of translanguaging has led to the creation of new theoretical constructs, such as translanguaging sub-spaces (Tai, 2023; Tai and Li Wei, 2023), trans-semiotising (Lin, 2015; Wu and Lin, 2019), transpositioning (Li and Lee, 2024; Tai, 2025a), transmodalities (Hawkins, 2018), transknowledging (Heugh, 2021), transprogramming (Tai, 2024a), transculturing (e.g., Lin and Chen, 2025; Lo, 2025) and transbordering (Xiao, 2025). Additionally, the section will present empirical evidence demonstrating how these constructs appear in various multilingual classroom settings to support the teaching and learning processes of both teachers and students.

#### 3.1.1 Transknowledging

The notion of transknowledging, introduced by Heugh (2021), refers to the 'informal and formal uses and practices of translanguaging alongside two-way exchange of knowledge systems' (p. 44). Heugh (2021) developed this notion through her research on remote communities in Sub-Saharan Africa, where she observed reciprocal exchanges of knowledge within Indigenous knowledge systems. She emphasizes the importance of societies valuing a balance among epistemology, ontology, and cosmology, and recognizing the significance of Indigenous knowledge systems, communal values, and the stewardship of land. This notion builds upon translanguaging, which Heugh (2021) described as primarily a linguistic process that has not adequately addressed the role of knowledge mediated by diverse meaning-making resources across time and space. Moreover, it challenges the unequal status of knowledge within the translanguaging space. Transknowledging, therefore, focuses on the processes of knowledge exchange and production, and it challenges the Eurocentrism that prevails in the global ecology of knowledge production. In other words, transknowledging challenges the privileges of dominant Western knowledge systems, advocating for the recognition and integration of diverse, often marginalized, knowledge systems from various cultural and epistemological backgrounds.

Transknowledging aligns with the principles of decoloniality by encouraging both students and teachers to draw upon the diverse knowledge systems of all students, rather than relying solely on Western concepts and knowledge. This approach allows students to utilize the varied knowledge they have gained through their cultural, communal, and Indigenous backgrounds. In doing so, they can actively participate in classroom learning, foster critical thinking, and facilitate meaningful knowledge exchange. However, it is important to note that the notion of translanguaging has also acknowledged speakers' role in mobilizing diverse multilingual and multimodal resources to bring diverse funds of knowledge into the social interactions (e.g., Tai and Li, 2020; Tai, 2022; Lin and Leung, 2024). As argued by Tai and Li (2020), creating a translanguaging space in a classroom can afford opportunities for teachers to bring their funds of knowledge to the forefront, thereby making academic content more relatable and meaningful to students' life experiences. Therefore, it is vital to note that Heugh's (2021) argument on transknowledging aligns with the notion of translanguaging as a theory of language (Li, 2018), which underscores the role of translanguaging in facilitating knowledge construction through social interaction. While translanguaging centres on the integrated use of a speaker's multilingual and multimodal resources for meaning-making, transknowledging specifically places an emphasis on valuing and incorporating non-dominant epistemologies in educational practices. This represents a deliberate decolonial move since the notion of transknowledging suggests that it is not enough to use home languages and personal experiences; educators must actively dismantle the privilege afforded to Western knowledge and create a genuine epistemic pluralism in the classroom. In essence, if translanguaging provides the mechanism for inclusive communication, transknowledging insists on a decolonial framework for that communication, ensuring it serves to rebalance power among the world's knowledge systems.

Studies (e.g., Heugh et al., 2022; Song, 2024) have demonstrated the role of transknowledging in supporting students' knowledge constructions in classroom interactions and promoting epistemic justice. Song (2024) investigated how teachers, tutors, and international students use translanguaging to decolonize the EMI curriculum, specifically focusing on knowledge related to Chinese philosophy and culture. Using nexus analysis as the methodological framework, the findings reveal that translanguaging facilitates transknowledging opportunities in the classroom, fostering negotiations among diverse discipline-specific knowledge systems. An analysis of tutorial sessions shows that the tutor's creation of a translanguaging space allows for transknowledging between Confucius' teachings, everyday expressions, and students' lived experiences. Notably, follow-up interviews with students indicate that dialogic exchanges with the tutor about Chinese philosophy help them perceive the continuity and relevance of ancient Chinese philosophers' thoughts in contemporary Chinese society. Song argues that translanguaging functions as a decolonial process of knowledge construction in EMI settings, enabling students to challenge the current unequal geopolitics of knowledge production. However, despite analysing various data sources, Song's study only examines one short extract of classroom interaction to demonstrate the manifestation of transknowledging in an EMI university classroom. This limitation suggests that further research with a broader range of classroom interactions is needed to fully understand the impact of transknowledging on students' knowledge construction during classroom interactions.

Heugh et al. (2022) investigated the role of human-language translation technology in reducing inequality and promoting inclusive teaching and learning practices for multilingual international students in Australia. Additionally, the study explores how this technology enables domestic and monolingual students and staff to access international knowledge and expertise. Data for the study were collected from various sources, including surveys, lesson materials used in tutorials, lecture recordings, and follow-up interviews with staff and students. The researchers implemented human-language translation technology interventions in courses such as Architecture, Applied Linguistics, English Language, Italian, and History. The findings suggest that human-language translation technology provides students with the opportunity to value knowledge from beyond Australia due to the additional perspectives it offers. This technology also helps students appreciate the diverse cultures and languages present in society. However, the study did not analyse teacher-student interactions during lectures or tutorials, limiting readers' understanding of how human-language translation technology supports the process of transknowledging at the classroom level to expand students' knowledge base.

### 3.1.2 Transmodalities

While translanguaging deconstructs boundaries between named languages, transmodalities (Hawkins, 2018) addresses the limitations of 'multimodality' by deconstructing the boundaries between all communicative modes. Hawkins argues that traditional multimodality often analyses modes (e.g., gaze, gesture, and image) in isolation. In contrast, transmodalities posits that these modes are inseparably intertwined; meaning emerges from their dynamic interplay and transformation across digital, local, and global contexts.

Hawkins (2018) introduced the concept of 'transmodalities', connected to critical cosmopolitanism, to emphasize the complexity and interconnectedness of modes that shape meaning in multimodal artefacts and communications. In her conceptualization, Hawkins outlined five complexities for analysing youths' transnational transmodal engagements in digital environments, which include 'modes intertwined', 'relationship between modes, language and material objects', 'production/assemblage, reception and negotiation', 'context and culture', and 'transnationalism and relations of power' (pp. 60–63). She argued that we must move beyond merely analysing the 'modes' of communication to considering 'a view of semiotic resources' (2018, p. 64), including modal movement and the transformation of these resources across local and global contexts, people and places, physical and digital spaces, and time. Hawkins' definition and framework of transmodalities prompt us to rethink the resources – such as place – that influence the engagement of youth and adult participants in digitally mediated communication. In essence, transmodalities facilitate the creation and sharing of meanings through multiple means and modes within, across, and through various contexts and cultures.

Hawkins (2018) further explained how the concept of transmodalities differs from the traditional understanding of 'multimodalities'. Jewitt (2014) defined multimodality as follows:

> Multimodality describes approaches that understand communication and representation to be more than about language, and which attend to the full range of communicational forms people use – image, gesture, gaze, posture and so on – and the relationships between these. (p. 15)

However, the concept of modes within the framework of 'multimodalities' has its limitations in terms of heuristic power. Firstly, work on modes often focuses on identifying specific modes (e.g., gaze or colour) and analysing their roles or meanings within a given interaction or set of interactions. In contrast, from the perspective of transmodalities, modes are intertwined and mutually constitute a message, making them inseparable. Based on the Global StoryBridges project conducted by Hawkins, she argues that messages and meanings are created through the interplay of modes used in videos, the text responses to them, and the discussions within sites, highlighting their inherently trans-modal nature. Additionally, the theorization of 'modes' from the perspective of multimodalities fails to account for the dynamics of power, privilege, and status that shape and are embedded in messages and their interpretations. This gap, therefore, motivated Hawkins to develop the concept of transmodalities (Hawkins, 2018). Thus, the crucial distinction between the notions of translanguaging and transmodalities is one of focus and framing. Translanguaging initiates a political project centred on the linguistic agency of multilingual individuals, while transmodalities pursues an analytical project that traces the semiotic flow of entire communicative ensembles, critically examining how power and culture shape this flow across transnational networks.

To date, there is a lack of studies exploring how transmodalities manifest at the classroom level to support students' knowledge construction and content and language learning (e.g., Bengochea et al., 2020; Sembiante et al., 2025). One of the few studies in this area, conducted by Sembiante et al. (2025), examined co-teachers' use of transmodalities in a dual language bilingual education preschool classroom. The researchers collected bi-weekly video recordings of co-teachers' morning cycle practices across three Spanish/English dual language bilingual education preschool classrooms to capture the transmodal interactions between teachers and students. The findings indicate that preschool co-teachers coordinated hybrid multimodal spaces and leveraged emergent bilingual children's transmodal expertise to explore visual, verbal, and actional forms of participation. The co-teachers created a ommunity of practice through coordinated, mirrored, and expanded transmodal practices. Their collaborative efforts engaged children in socially aligned (e.g., modelling participation norms, promoting engagement) and instructionally relevant (e.g., fostering numeracy and literacy) routines and purposes of morning cycles. Although Sembiante et al. (2025) demonstrated the benefits of teachers' transmodalities for expanding emergent bilingual learners' semiotic repertoires and reaffirming their multimodal communicative choices, the analysis did not address how power relations might influence or obstruct opportunities for teachers and emergent bilinguals to utilize different multimodal resources to facilitate meaning-making processes. Consequently, there remains a gap in understanding the full impact of power dynamics on the accessibility of transmodal practices in multilingual education settings.

### 3.1.3 Trans-Semiotising

The notion of trans-semiotising was introduced by Lin (2015) and emphasized the need to understand how language (as one semiotic resource) and other semiotics, such as gestures, visuals, sound, and music, interact and intertwine in human communication. While both translanguaging and trans-semiotising capture fluid, whole-body meaning-making, Lemke and Lin (2022) argued that the two concepts have slightly different focuses. Translanguaging highlights the 'deployment of a speaker's full linguistic repertoire' (Otheguy et al., 2015, p. 3) for thinking and communication, whereas trans-semiotising considers 'non-speech actions, non-speech events, physical responses of non-human mediums, and in general all processes and flows that contribute to the unfolding of an activity' (Lemke and Lin, 2022, p. 136). Therefore, trans-semiotising strongly emphasizes multimodality. Lin (2015) seeks to expand the scope of translanguaging to explore the intricate interplay of language with a wide array of semiotic components, all contributing to the complex process of meaning construction.

While the notion of trans-semiotising (Lin, 2015) is often aligned with translanguaging, a critical distinction lies in their theoretical origins and primary objects of study, which creates a subtle but significant boundary. Translanguaging emerged from bilingual education and critical sociolinguistics, fundamentally challenging the political construct of 'named languages' to focus on a speaker's unified linguistic repertoire. In contrast, trans-semiotising originates in social semiotics and systemic functional linguistics, aiming to dethrone language itself from its privileged position by analysing its seamless integration with other semiotic resources like gesture, image, and sound (Lemke and Lin, 2022). These two notions reveal a difference in theoretical commitment. Translanguaging starts with the multilingual speaker and their political struggle against monolingualism, expanding outward to include multimodality. Trans-semiotising starts with the multimodal ensemble of communication and analyses how language functions as one component within it. This distinction highlights a key tension. Translanguaging's primary goal is a political one: to liberate multilingual practices from the constraints of 'named languages'. An overemphasis on trans-semiotising risks side-lining this goal by absorbing language into a wider, and less politically charged, study of all signs and symbols. Thus, I argue that Li's (2018) incorporation of a multimodal perspective into translanguaging can be seen as a strategic theoretical expansion, co-opting the analytical power of trans-semiotising while ensuring the focus remains firmly on the agency and linguistic resources of the multilingual individual.

Li (2018) further argued that translanguaging embraces the multimodal social semiotic perspective that linguistic signs are part of a broader repertoire of modal resources available to sign makers, carrying particular socio-historical and political associations. It highlights the various ways language users employ, create, and interpret different kinds of signs to communicate across contexts and participants and to perform their different subjectivities.

To date, numerous studies have examined how trans-semiotising manifests in multilingual classrooms to support students' content and second language (L2) learning (e.g., Ollerhead, 2018; Wu and Lin, 2019; Liu, 2020; Gu et al., 2022; An and Zheng, 2024). Wu and Lin's (2019) study is among the earliest to explore trans-semiotising practices in a secondary Grade 10 CLIL biology class in Hong Kong, focusing on the topic of transpiration. The study's findings show that multiple linguistic and semiotic resources were mobilized during three core lesson stages: exploring and defining transpiration, investigating the phenomenon and drawing diagrams and notes, and entextualizing the experience and explaining. This involved the dynamic blending of students' everyday Cantonese, scientific terms in English (e.g., diffusion, evaporation, osmosis), laboratory experiences (e.g., observing vegetable stems and leaves), drawings related to scientific phenomena (e.g., plant and cell diagrams), and the teacher's talk, gestures, and vocalizations. Wu and Lin's (2019) analysis demonstrates that all available linguistic and semiotic resources were seamlessly integrated in the meaning-making process, co-contributed by the teacher and students, enabling students to expand and transform students' communicative repertoires to construct and communicate scientific knowledge of transpiration pull.

Liu (2020) analysed discourse in secondary EMI humanities classrooms in Hong Kong to examine how translanguaging and trans-semiotising facilitate content and language learning. The findings indicate that these processes support the co-construction of general and subject-specific English lexical knowledge and skills in academic English writing. Students integrated visual language with written language to express their feelings and meanings in written assignments, challenging traditional distinctions between academic (formal writing) and non-academic registers (e.g., drawing). This also contested the ideology that old visual literacy (calligraphic language) is more valuable than new visual literacy, which includes a mix of texts, images, sounds, and colours. Liu recommended that teachers use translanguaging and trans-semiotising as scaffolding strategies to support students' creation of new knowledge and to empower their thinking and sense of self-worth.

### 3.1.4 Transpositioning

Research on translanguaging has led to the development of the concept of transpositioning in Applied Linguistics. Based on positioning theory (Davies and Harre, 1990) and liquid modernity (Bauman, 2012 [2000]), transpositioning refers to 'the multiple and interwoven layers of positioning involved in all communicative endeavours' (Hawkins, 2022, p. 3). Liquid modernity suggests a natural tendency towards continuous change, emphasizing the dynamic nature of language use. Speakers utilize various linguistic resources and modes, blending them within a semiotic repertoire to create innovative and/or critical interventions. Transpositioning involves individuals stepping out of their established roles and adopting different viewpoints through translanguaging. By challenging traditional norms and embracing a wider range of possibilities, transpositioning enables individuals to break free from conventional thinking and develop empathy for others in the process (Li and Lee, 2024). Viewing identity as a continuous process of altering one's position and that of others, transpositioning highlights the dynamic nature of social interactions, where speakers adjust their identity positions in response to the evolving interaction. Essentially, transpositioning demonstrates how speakers free themselves from fixed roles or positions in social interactions and navigate their stance while engaging with other conversation partners.

Notably, Tai's study (2025a) is the first to expand on the concept of transpositioning introduced by Li (2024) and Li and Lee (2024), focusing on how it occurs in teacher-student classroom interactions. The study explores how a teacher engages in transpositioning by adopting various positions to create imaginary scenarios and participate in mutual learning with students. Building on previous work (Tai and Li, 2021a; Tai and Li, 2023), Tai argued that the co-learning process can be seen as a transpositioning process, requiring the teacher to strategically and iteratively shift their stance and social roles from a knowledge provider to a knowledge recipient. These shifts help construct new meanings in classroom interactions and enhance students' content knowledge learning. Tai (2025a) emphasized the importance of translanguaging practices in facilitating transpositioning, allowing speakers to free themselves from fixed roles and adjust their stance during conversations. Consequently, adopting the concepts of translanguaging and transpositioning as analytical perspectives could enable researchers to examine how speakers alter their roles, stances, and positions through translanguaging to achieve specific communicative goals in social interactions.

Tai and Lee (2023) further explored the significance of transpositioning by exploring how a CAL teacher creates a safe translanguaging space for co-learning, which allows him to alleviate ethnic minority students' anxiety in learning CAL. Using Multimodal Conversation Analysis and Interpretative Phenomenological Analysis, the analysis shows that the teacher and students switch seamlessly between Cantonese and English, adopting and alternating roles as learners and teachers, while using various gestures to facilitate communication. Building on these findings, the authors propose the concept of Transpositioning-Translanguaging-Co-learning. This heuristic helps educators create an equitable and supportive learning environment by reshaping traditional teacher-student power dynamics. In the CAL context, it involves teachers fluidly transitioning between different discursive identities during classroom interactions to achieve pedagogical goals. Translanguaging facilitates transpositioning by freeing participants from the constraints of fixed linguistic identities, lowering their insecurity about role shifts, and encouraging a transpositioning mindset. The outcome is a co-learning approach that reduces ethnic minority students' anxiety in CAL learning. The Transpositioning-Translanguaging-Co-Learning framework addresses the sociopsychological context, pedagogical strategies, and educational outcomes needed to balance power dynamics in the classroom, fostering an inclusive environment where teachers and students engage in a bi-directional learning and teaching process.

This approach helps alleviate foreign language anxiety by making students feel more comfortable and less intimidated by the teacher's authority.

### 3.1.5 Translanguaging Sub-Spaces

Tai's (2023) monograph advances the theory of translanguaging space (Li, 2011) by proposing that multilingual classrooms can be seen as integrated translanguaging spaces composed of fluid and dynamic translanguaging sub-spaces. These sub-spaces allow participants to blend various linguistic, multimodal, and sociocultural resources to enhance teaching and learning. Tai (2023) suggests that breaking down the concept of 'translanguaging space' into different sub-spaces can help researchers identify the subtleties within the broader construct, emphasizing its dynamic nature (Tai and Li, 2025). This aligns with Seedhouse's (2004) argument that classroom interaction is composed of distinct sub-varieties, such as form and accuracy contexts, meaning and fluency contexts, task-oriented contexts, and procedural contexts. Prior research on classroom interaction has often focused on specific action types (e.g., Markee, 1995; Morell, 2007) and interactional structures (e.g., Lee, 2007), portraying teachers as addressing one pedagogical action at a time. However, Seedhouse (2004) demonstrated that L2 teachers may simultaneously focus on multiple pedagogical goals, with classroom interaction occurring on several levels at once. Thus, analysing classroom interaction requires considering the specific context to avoid acontextual overgeneralizations. Building on Seedhouse's (2004) argument, Tai (2023) argued that multilingual classrooms should not be viewed as static, invariant translanguaging spaces, but rather as integrated spaces comprising multiple sub-spaces. These sub-spaces enable teachers to utilize specific resources in a coordinated manner to achieve their pedagogical goals at different moments during the classroom interaction.

Examples of multiple translanguaging sub-spaces include, a co-learning space (Tai and Li, 2021a), a space for integrating outside knowledge into the classroom (Tai and Li, 2020), a space for playful talk (Tai and Li, 2021b), a technology-mediated translanguaging space (Tai and Li, 2024), and a space for facilitating cross-curricular connections (Tai, 2024b). In their theoretical paper on task-based language teaching, East and Wang (2024) contended that existing research offers limited insight into incorporating translanguaging into the pre-, during-, and post-task phases of L2 instruction. They propose that within the task-based language teaching framework, different tasks and lesson phases, such as pre-task and post-task, can be viewed as translanguaging sub-spaces. These overarching and specific sub-spaces enable translanguaging in task-based language teaching, potentially reshaping existing practices that are centred around target-language-oriented task-based practices.

Additionally, Tai and Li (2025) provided empirical evidence in order to demonstrate how an EMI classroom's translanguaging space can be divided into different sub-spaces: one at the whole-class level and another at the individual level. To establish a translanguaging sub-space at the whole-class level, the teacher should consider all students rather than just the majority or minority during translanguaging practices in classroom activities, ensuring that learning is accessible to everyone. At the individual level, the teacher should use translanguaging to engage students with specific learning challenges, providing them with equal access to educational opportunities and enabling their full participation in the context of whole-class instruction. Tai and Li argue that the process of engaging students in content learning is inherently a translanguaging process, requiring teachers to utilize their available resources to create these diverse sub-spaces. This approach addresses the varied needs of students, enhances their academic achievement, and promotes interaction and inclusion within the classroom.

Apart from face-to-face classroom environment, Ho and Tai (2024) investigated the complexities of translanguaging space within the online context of YouTube. They view YouTube as a broad translanguaging space that allows for the creation of various sub-spaces. By analysing two videos specifically chosen from the same YouTube channel, they identified two distinct, but interconnected translanguaging sub-spaces formed through teaching English vocabulary on the platform: an interactional translanguaging space and a performative translanguaging space. The interactional space is crafted through teachers' use of linguistic resources like different registers and speaking styles, along with multimodal resources such as gestures, body movements, onscreen text, and background music, all utilized in role plays for teaching vocabulary. The performative space emerges from the comments made by both teachers and learners, which allow them to reposition themselves to construct and negotiate knowledge. Ho and Tai (2024) not only addressed Tai and Li's (2025) point that the complexities of translanguaging space are underexplored (Tai, 2023; Tai and Li, 2025), but also illustrated how these translanguaging sub-spaces can leverage the complete range of resources from both students and teachers for meaning-making and self-expression on online platforms.

### 3.1.6 Transprogramming

The concept of transprogramming (Tai, 2024a) describes the ability to strategically orchestrate a unified repertoire that integrates natural languages, multimodal resources, and the syntactic and logical structures of programming languages to complete computational tasks and generate new meanings. This notion recognizes that effective interaction with technology – especially in the era of generative artificial intelligence (AI) – is not a monolingual act but a dynamic, translingual, and trans-semiotic process. As AI transforms global communication and knowledge work, the ability to 'think with' and 'speak to' machines becomes a fundamental literacy. This goes beyond writing traditional code; it encompasses the entire ecosystem of human-AI interaction, including crafting effective prompts, interpreting AI-generated outputs, and debugging computational logic. In this context, programming languages and AI interfaces function as potent semiotic systems (Vogel et al., 2019, 2020; Radke et al., 2020), and transprogramming is the practice of weaving these systems with one's other linguistic and multimodal resources. This fusion is crucial for developing computational literacies, which entails students' capacity in co-creating and critically evaluating content with AI. Therefore, transprogramming positions multilinguals not just as a passive user of technology, but as an empowered agent who can leverage their full repertoire to navigate, command, and shape the digital world.

Transprogramming differs from translanguaging in its focus and application. While translanguaging, as defined by Li (2018), emphasizes using diverse linguistic and multimodal resources for human communication, transprogramming extends this to interactions with programming tasks, which require strict adherence to formal languages and rules. Embracing transprogramming involves using various linguistic, semiotic, and computer-based resources dynamically and strategically, allowing classroom participants to enhance programming skills and foster creative problem-solving. Tai (2024a) provided empirical evidence of how an IT teacher in a Hong Kong primary school uses multilingual, multimodal, and programming resources to aid students in programming tasks. The analysis shows that the IT teacher employs various linguistic, semiotic, and technological strategies to teach programming. This includes using hypothetical scenarios to explain programming concepts and offering step-by-step instructions to help students improve their debugging skills. By blending multilingual and multimodal resources, the teacher aims to enhance students' understanding of programming concepts and empower them in programming discourse. Hence, the notion of transprogramming emphasizes that while programming code is essential for expressing computational logic, other linguistic and semiotic resources play a role in enhancing students' grasp of programming concepts. Thus, embracing transprogramming enables teachers and students to use their entire repertoire to develop creative problem-solving strategies and facilitate human-machine communication.

### 3.1.7 Transbordering

The notion of transbordering, introduced by Xiao (2025), illuminates a specific dimension of communicative practice. It is defined as 'a semiotic process in which individuals create, negotiate, and contest boundaries that define acceptable academic practices, identities, and modes of communication' (p. 1). This concept introduces a necessary tension: while translanguaging as a political act seeks to deconstruct oppressive linguistic borders, Xiao argued that bordering – the act of creating conceptual distinctions – remains an essential cognitive and pedagogical tool for making sense of the world. This positions transbordering as a vital complement to translanguaging. Although translanguaging highlights the inherent fluidity of semiotic resources, it is the socially constructed boundaries – shaped by policies, ideologies, and norms of interaction – that give this fluidity significance within educational and political contexts. Conversely, transbordering focuses on how these boundaries become perceptible, are navigated, and can be reshaped during meaning-making processes. Rather than contradicting translanguaging, transbordering extends its approach by concentrating on the spatial and semiotic practices that actively negotiate boundaries during social interactions.

Xiao's (2025) study demonstrates this relationship by analysing interactions in an English-dominant graduate course. Drawing on Multimodal CA as the methodological framework, he shows that even within a 'single' language, participants engage in dynamic meaning-making. For instance, an instructor might create a clear conceptual border between 'applied' and 'theoretical' linguistics (a transbordering act) to scaffold understanding, but do so by orchestrating diverse linguistic, semiotic, and spatial resources (a translanguaging practice) to bridge students' prior knowledge with new academic concepts. This illustrates that transbordering does not oppose translanguaging but complements it; bordering can be a strategic means to enable more effective translanguaging and knowledge integration.

Xiao's (2025) findings advance translanguaging pedagogy by revealing that boundary-making and boundary-crossing are not contradictory, but often simultaneous and interdependent processes. The instructor creates instructional borders to clarify content while simultaneously transcending linguistic borders to include diverse perspectives. Thus, transbordering enriches our understanding of the translanguaging space (Li, 2011) by theorizing how the negotiation of boundaries themselves is a central mechanism through which new knowledge and identities are co-constructed.

### 3.1.8 Transculturing

The notion of transculturing builds upon 'transcultural communication' (Baker and Sangiamchit, 2019), which emerged as a critical response to the term 'intercultural communication'. Whereas intercultural communication often treats cultures as separate, bounded entities, transcultural communication rejects this static 'in-between' model (Baker and Ishikawa, 2019). Instead, it emphasizes the fluid movement through and across cultural and linguistic boundaries, challenging the very idea of 'named' cultures and languages as stable, independent systems. This perspective is fundamentally aligned with translanguaging theory (Li, 2018). Just as translanguaging posits that speakers dynamically draw on their full linguistic and semiotic repertoires without regard for named-language boundaries, transcultural communication recognizes that individuals similarly synthesize and traverse cultural resources. Together, the notion of transcultural communication reframes communication not as an interaction between pre-defined categories, but as a dynamic, integrated process where language, culture, and modality are simultaneously mobilized to create new meanings.

Building on this theoretical foundation, transculturing is defined as the process through which multilinguals mobilize their full repertoires to integrate cultural perspectives that transcend traditional boundaries, thereby fostering a deeper understanding of diversity (Lin and Chen, 2025). This concept has been further theorized by Lo (2025), who investigates how culture is continuously relocated and redefined through human imagination and productivity. Analysing social media posts related to the Korean Wave fandom, Lo argues that transculturing is a 'situated process through which cultural materials, meanings, and practices are relocated, recontextualized, and remade as they move across diverse social, linguistic, and semiotic environments' (p. 22).

Despite these robust theoretical developments, a significant gap remains in their application to classroom discourse. To date, no empirical studies have examined how teachers enact transculturing in situ – that is, how they mobilize their full semiotic repertoires during classroom interactions to foster students' critical understanding of linguistic and cultural diversity. Consequently, there is a pressing need for classroom interactional data to illustrate how the dynamic process of transculturing is concretely manifested and pedagogically leveraged in multilingual classrooms.

## 3.2 Summary

This section presents empirical evidence to illustrate new concepts developed by translanguaging scholars, such as translanguaging sub-spaces, trans-semiotising, transpositioning, transmodalities, transknowledging, transprogramming, transculturing, and transbordering. These concepts share a common thread in emphasizing the value of the 'trans' prefix by highlighting fluid practices that go beyond socially established language systems and structures. Translanguaging scholars use translanguaging as an analytical perspective to reconceptualize existing theories, shifting researchers' focus towards investigating multiple meaning-making systems and subjectivities. They also explore the transdisciplinary implications of redefining translanguaging's role in various academic fields, including linguistics, education, and computer science. The next section will concentrate on different methodological approaches to studying the complexities of translanguaging practices in classroom discourse.

## 4 Researching Translanguaging in Classroom Interactions

## 4.1 Methodological Approaches for Studying Translanguaging

This section examines various methods for investigating translanguaging in classroom discourse: Critical Discourse Analysis (CDA), Conversation Analysis (CA), Linguistic Ethnography (LE), Moment Analysis, and the combination of Multimodal CA with Interpretative Phenomenological Analysis (IPA). It will also discuss empirical evidence showcasing how researchers use these approaches to study translanguaging in multilingual classrooms.

### 4.1.1 Critical Discourse Analysis

CDA is a qualitative methodology designed to investigate the interplay between power and language, as well as other modes of communication (Kress, 1997; Fairclough, 2013). CDA researchers consider discourse a significant form of social practice that both reproduces and transforms knowledge, identities, and social relations, including power dynamics, while simultaneously being shaped by other social practices and structures (Jørgensen and Philips, 2002). Given that social interaction is deeply intertwined with the political, social, and cultural practices, CDA can be utilized to uncover inequalities and power structures in educational settings. Jenks (2020) also highlighted that many studies on classroom discourse have adopted an uncritical perspective, potentially limiting the effectiveness of classroom discourse analysis as a means to challenge power dynamics in educational environments. In a similar vein, Kimura and Tsai (2023) emphasized the importance of employing CDA to analyse classroom discourse in order to comprehend how classroom interactions are influenced by a range of factors, including institutional policies and goals at the meso-level and broader social ideologies concerning language and knowledge at the macro-level.

Fairclough (2013) provided frameworks and tools for analysing classroom interactions, arguing that 'relations of power are actually exercised and enacted' within discourse (p. 36). He differentiated between 'power in' and 'power behind' discourse. Power in discourse pertains to how power is evident in conversations among individuals from different groups and positionalities, as well as in the mass media. On the other hand, power behind discourse highlights 'how orders of discourse, as dimensions of the social orders of social institutions or societies, are themselves shaped and constituted by relations of power' (p. 36). Essentially, the power behind discourse examines how ideological and institutional structures and conflicts influence the dynamics of classroom interactions.

Methodologically, CDA involves describing, interpreting, and explaining spoken and written texts as they interact within broader ethnographic discursive contexts (Fairclough, 2003). Researchers engage in CDA by: (1) *describing* the use of linguistic and multimodal resources in the discourse, (2) *interpreting* the reasons for employing these resources, and (3) *explaining* the complex relationships between participants' use of linguistic and various communicative cues within the discourse, along with the sociocultural, institutional, and historical contexts in which the discourse occurs. Fairclough (2003) identifies three contexts: local, institutional, and societal. *The local context* refers to the immediate setting of the interaction, such as a classroom. *The institutional context* encompasses the norms and policies of social institutions that shape the local environment. *The societal context* involves broader governmental policies and mandates that impact both local and institutional contexts. CDA's focus on exploring the role of language and other semiotic resources in perpetuating ideologically sustained power relations allows it to provide a thorough, context-sensitive critique of how linguistic and multimodal resources both shape and mirror power dynamics in education.

The process for doing CDA begins with data collection, which includes collecting recordings and transcriptions of classroom discourse, as well as collecting contextual details about the institutional and pedagogical environment. Researchers then conduct preliminary observations to identify interactional patterns such as turn-taking dynamics and dominant speakers. At the micro-level, linguistic features like lexical choices, grammar, and speech acts are analysed to uncover implicit power relations. The meso-level focuses on discursive practices, including framing and intertextuality, while the macro-level examines broader social and ideological influences, such as institutional power and cultural hegemony. The final stage involves interpreting the data by revisiting previous stages and making analytic notes to draw comprehensive conclusions.

There are a considerable number of studies that employ CDA as a methodological framework to examine how classroom translanguaging practices either challenge or reinforce power relations and ideologies (e.g., Sah and Li, 2022; Qin and Llosa, 2023; Rajendram, 2023; Shepard-Carey, 2023). Among these, Shepard-Carey's (2023) study is one of the first to use CDA to thoroughly analyse how teachers' translanguaging practices impact student engagement in primary-level EAL classrooms in the US and how it influences or limits L2 learning opportunities. The study reveals that while teachers use translanguaging to aid students' comprehension, they often rely on direct translations and limited questioning, which does not promote extended student interaction or elaboration. This unequal power dynamic is evident, as it reflects traditional authoritative teacher roles that restrict multilingual students' ability to make sense of the material and engage in dialogue. The study underscores the importance for teachers to critically assess their translanguaging practices to ensure they create spaces that encourage student elaboration and exploration across various languages.

Sah and Li (2022) adopted CDA to study the language use of teachers and students in EMI classrooms at a multilingual secondary school in Nepal. Most students speak Newari, an indigenous language, as their first language, with others coming from Nepali, Gurung, and Limbu-speaking communities. The authors gather data through classroom observations, teacher interviews, and student focus group discussions to explore translanguaging practices in these classrooms. The analysis of classroom interactions shows that translanguaging between English and Nepali helps facilitate student participation and comprehension to some extent. However, the authors argue that the uncritical adoption of translanguaging by teachers and students reinforces the hierarchy of named languages, privileging national languages, like Nepali, over indigenous languages, such as Newari, for minoritized students. They introduce the concept of 'unequal languaging', suggesting that these practices create a discriminatory learning environment for linguistically marginalized children. The study emphasizes the importance for EMI teachers to critically engage in translanguaging and promote the equal integration of minoritized languages. This perspective is echoed by Rajendram (2023), who notes that students' language choices in multilingual classrooms are influenced by ethnic and national discourses and the political and ethnic tensions surrounding them. Therefore, researchers should not assume that translanguaging functions uniformly across different social, cultural, and political contexts, but should instead carefully consider the unique characteristics, opportunities, and limitations of translanguaging in each specific context.

Qin and Llosa (2023) investigated the benefits and challenges of translanguaging pedagogy in a multilingual secondary science classroom in the US. Using CDA to examine classroom interactions, they identify five beneficial functions of translanguaging pedagogy: translingual support, translingual caring, translingual critical love, translingual bonding, and translingual safe houses. They also identify two challenging aspects: translingual exclusion and translingual aggression. The analysis reveals that translanguaging provides opportunities for teachers and students to negotiate meaning and build relationships. However, it also shows that students sometimes use translanguaging for exclusion and aggression, including misogynistic and racist behaviours. The study underscores the complexity of translanguaging pedagogy and suggests that researchers should adopt a nuanced perspective that acknowledges both its affordances and challenges (e.g., Charalambous et al., 2016; Allard, 2017; Rajendram, 2023).

The studies by Sah and Li (2022), Shepard-Carey (2023), and Qin and Llosa (2023) emphasize the importance of examining how power and ideology intersect with translanguaging practices in classrooms. Using CDA as a methodological framework allows researchers to develop a more critical approach to translanguaging pedagogy, promoting educational equity for multilingual students. However, most of these studies, with the exception of Shepard-Carey's (2023), tend to view translanguaging simply as switching between named languages (e.g., Sah and Li, 2022; Qin and Llosa, 2023), and their discourse analysis is often brief and not fine-grained. This contrasts with Conversation Analytic studies (e.g., Lin and Wu, 2015; Bozbiyik and Morton, 2025; Tai and Dai, 2024), which provide detailed analyses of classroom interactions using multimodal transcriptions to illustrate translanguaging across various modalities. By doing so, CA researchers aim to uncover the complexity of translanguaging practices, demonstrating how teachers and students engage with multiple meaning-making systems to create new configurations of language and pedagogical practices.

### 4.1.2 Conversation Analysis

CA rooted in ethnomethodology and sociology examines how members of a social group collaboratively construct social order through detailed analysis of social interactions (Brouwer and Wagner, 2004). It adopts a participant-focused approach to reveal the intricate processes by which social actions, such as learning, are organized and accomplished through conversation. CA enables researchers to study naturally occurring interactions, considering every small detail crucial for understanding participants' perspectives on the interaction. Researchers are encouraged to avoid preconceived notions about the significance of language in use, including semiotic elements like eye contact and gestures. The focus should be on interaction sequences rather than isolated exchanges or turns (Hutchby and Wooffitt, 1998). A fundamental aspect of CA is its view of interaction as systematically organized. Heritage (1995) highlighted that social interactions are shaped by established structural practices to which participants are typically oriented, indicating that interactions follow recognizable patterns that participants adhere to during conversations.

Through 'empirically based accounts of the observable conversational behaviours of participants' (Markee, 2005, p. 355), research in CA has identified several formal features of conversation, such as turn-taking, adjacency pairs, repair mechanisms, and preferred versus dispreferred organizations (ten Have, 2007). These interactional elements provide a valuable foundation for researchers analysing conversations across various social settings. However, as Richards (2006, p. 13) pointed out, the focus of analysis should not be on whether participants strictly follow these rules, but on how they collaboratively construct the conversation and develop a mutual understanding of its context. CA analysts should focus on how the conversation progresses rather than examining individual utterances in isolation. Therefore, when analysing interactions turn-by-turn, it is essential to transcribe the spoken dialogue meticulously, capturing details like pauses, pitch, and pace, with 'a ferocious attention to detail that not all researchers can muster' (Richards, 2003, p. 28). This approach is crucial because the way social interactions are constructed provides as much insight into meaning and context as the content itself.

The analysis of naturally occurring audio and video data in CA begins with the principle of 'unmotivated' looking. This means that researchers should establish their research focus based solely on the recorded interactions, without considering external factors not acknowledged by the participants, to develop an insider (emic) understanding of classroom interactions. While some might argue that all observations have inherent motivations (e.g., Psathas, 1995), the intention is for researchers to initially examine the data without a specific focus, allowing for an open exploration before conducting further analysis. Thus, it's crucial for researchers to approach the video data without preconceived notions, such as expecting translanguaging practices to appear. When identifying translanguaging practices, researchers compile collections of similar instances and examine both the differences and similarities between cases to uncover various aspects or features of these practices (Sidnell, 2010).

Line-by-line analysis is used to study how conversation is organized sequentially, examining each turn in relation to the preceding and following utterances. To ensure the analysis is reliable, researchers use the next turn proof procedure and consider participant orientation to validate their claims (Tai, 2022). This means analysts must base their observations on the participants' visible orientations and understandings. To prevent CA analyses from being influenced by ethnographic information from participants or the researcher's perspective as a participant observer, any analytical claims about the classroom data must be supported by details from the interaction itself (Seedhouse, 2004). This approach aligns with the CA goal of examining 'what is publicly transacted, not what is privately thought or felt' (Antaki, 2012, p. 9).

An increasing number of studies are using CA to explore the complexities of translanguaging practices in classroom discourse (e.g., Lin and Wu, 2015; Jakonen et al., 2018; Ou and Gu, 2022; Bozbiyik and Morton, 2025; Zuo and Walsh, 2023; Lin and Leung, 2024; Nikula et al., 2024; Tai and Dai, 2024; Tian, 2024; Zhang et al., 2025). Lin and Wu's (2015) study is, to the best of my knowledge, the first to utilize CA to examine how learners employ translanguaging to actively construct meaning and demonstrate understanding in a year 8 Hong Kong EMI science classroom. Their analysis of a five-minute classroom interaction reveals that the teacher predominantly adheres to the rigid Initiation-Response-Feedback pattern and does not engage the students' first language, Cantonese, to facilitate their access to English-language science discourse. However, when the teacher allows a low-proficiency learner to respond in Cantonese, it enables the learner to initiate a longer sequence in Cantonese, contrasting her earlier struggle to articulate responses in English. The authors suggest that providing space for learners to translanguage by using their familiar linguistic resources, including both everyday and academic language, can effectively support their learning of L2 science discourse.

Bozbiyik and Morton (2025) expanded on Bonacina-Pugh's (2012) concept of practiced language policy to explore how a university lecturer uses multilingual, multimodal, and interactional resources in an EMI postgraduate pharmacology course at a Spanish university for meaning-making and to determine the overall medium of interaction in the classroom. They employ multimodal CA as their methodological framework to identify the structured nature of the interaction, focusing on the shifts between explaining core content and addressing other pedagogical goals, which complement the content itself. The findings reveal that, although the stated medium of instruction is L2 English, the actual medium of instruction practiced is bilingual, involving both L1 Spanish and L2 English. The authors argue that translanguaging serves as the medium of instruction in this EMI setting. By utilizing a variety of interactional, multimodal, and linguistic resources, such as culturally specific embodied actions and colloquial Spanish expressions, the lecturer creates a translanguaging space that allows students to integrate their personal histories, experiences, identities, and emotions into the process of building disciplinary knowledge. The authors emphasize that translanguaging can be used by teachers to connect target content knowledge with the shared community of teachers and students in the classroom. This study also supports the notion of practiced language policy (Bonacina-Pugh, 2012), which emphasizes how the legitimacy of a particular language is negotiated at the local level of classroom interaction and is followed by other participants in the classroom.

Nikula et al. (2024) explored how the unpacking and repacking of disciplinary knowledge is accomplished multimodally in Finnish CLIL Physics and Chemistry classrooms through translanguaging practices. The study combines multimodal CA with Legitimation Code Theory to emphasize the complexity involved in constructing knowledge. The research findings indicate that teachers employ various multimodal resources, including depictive gestures, everyday objects, and pedagogical tools such as PowerPoint, Prezi presentations, smartboards, and inscriptions, to break down subject-specific knowledge. The authors suggest that these varied multimodal resources allow teachers to engage in multimodal translanguaging, facilitating the construction and communication of subject-specific meanings. This finding is consistent with Tai's (2024d) study, which demonstrates that EMI teachers' translanguaging practices help convert student contributions into academic terminology and concepts. The use of translanguaging to transform student contributions highlights its importance as a component of teachers' classroom interactional competence, crucial for developing new language practice configurations and achieving specific pedagogical goals. This also illustrates how translanguaging, as both a theory of language and a process of knowledge construction, can be enhanced by incorporating insights from other areas of the social sciences.

The cited studies (e.g., Lin and Wu, 2015; Bozbiyik and Morton, 2025; Nikula et al., 2024) have demonstrated that CA is effective in detailing how translanguaging practices are collaboratively constructed between teachers and students in EMI/CLIL classrooms, even though classroom participants are expected to use the target language (English) throughout the lessons under a monolingual policy. Specifically, research on translanguaging in multilingual classrooms (e.g., Ou and Gu, 2022; Bozbiyik and Morton, 2025; Nikula et al., 2024) has shown how translanguaging operates across different modalities using multimodal transcriptions. CA focuses on the details of talk, considering how a specific aspect of context is deemed relevant by the interlocutors and affects the interaction's progression. This perspective is often critiqued as being too narrow (e.g., Matsumoto, 2018), as CA analysis does not allow researchers to examine how factors like power, political issues, gender, and ethnicity shape social interactions. In other words, CA cannot reveal how participants' personal histories, ideologies, and beliefs contribute to creating translanguaging spaces in classrooms (Tai, 2023). Therefore, ethnographic information from interviews and participant observations should be combined with detailed moment-by-moment analysis of talk-in-interaction. This will be further discussed in Section 4.2.

### 4.1.3 Linguistic Ethnography

LE is a methodology that combines linguistics and ethnography to conduct detailed studies of social interactions within specific contexts. This approach aims to understand the social processes individuals are involved in (Rampton, 2007) and how these interactions are situated within broader social structures and communicative contexts. LE is shaped by interpretive approaches drawn from fields such as applied linguistics, sociology, cultural studies, and anthropology. While influenced by established methods, LE asserts its own initiative. It has been suggested that LE benefits from established theories by 'making wider connections, drawing attention to neglected issues' (Tusting and Maybin, 2007, p. 575). LE enables researchers to emphasize the reciprocal relationship between language and social life. This is illustrated in Rampton et al.'s (2004, p. 2) explanation that 'language and social life are mutually shaping, and that close analysis of situated language use can provide both fundamental and distinctive insights into the mechanisms and dynamics of social and cultural production in everyday activity'. Rampton (2007, p. 585) further outlined two principles for the development of LE: (1) 'meaning takes shape within specific social relations, interactional histories, and institutional regimes, produced and construed by agents with expectations and repertoires that have to be grasped ethnographically'; and (2) 'meaning is far more than just an 'expression of ideas'; it encompasses biography, identification, stance, and nuance extensively signalled in the linguistic and textual fine-grain'. Therefore, LE views meaning-making as a complex discursive practice in social interactions, shaped by multiple sociocultural factors, including individuals' sociocultural experiences, identities, beliefs, and social contexts, which influence or limit their linguistic choices.

LE offers the possibility of combining linguistic analysis (such as CA or CDA) with ethnographic methods, allowing each to complement the other's strengths and mitigate their weaknesses (Rampton, 2007). Linguistic ethnographers utilize a variety of analytic tools for data collection and analysis, including conducting ethnographic interviews for data collection and employing CA for data analysis. These tools are drawn from both ethnographic and linguistic traditions. As Rampton et al. (2004, p. 596) noted, 'Ethnography opens Linguistics up, inviting reflexive sensitivity to the processes involved in the production of linguistic claims and to the potential importance of what gets left out'. By using rich descriptions, audio/video data, a range of ethnographic interview data, and other textual documents, researchers can gain a better understanding of how language is used in ongoing communicative activities and situated social actions, and what this reveals about broader social constraints, structures, and ideologies (Copland and Creese, 2015). Conducting LE involves combining 'open ethnographic observations' (Copland and Creese, 2015, p. 37) with detailed linguistic analysis, typically through participant observation. Since a participant observer inevitably influences the context in some way, validity is sought not by avoiding this influence but through reflexivity and acknowledging one's role in producing the data (Rampton, 2007).

Despite the complementary nature of the two elements in LE, they can sometimes pull in different directions. Reconciling the emic, bottom-up approach of ethnography (Hammersley and Atkinson, 2007) with the etic framework in linguistics, such as CDA, which tends to have a realist orientation, can be challenging. Additionally, although CA employs an emic approach to understand participants' orientations in social interactions, several CA scholars (e.g., Antaki, 2012; Ford, 2012) have highlighted issues with combining CA and ethnography. There is no straightforward solution to these tensions, as it largely depends on the researchers' choices of linguistic frameworks and ethnographic methods, and how they reconcile the differing ontological and epistemological assumptions underlying their selections. Nonetheless, LE can be applied to various research projects that explore the interactions between language, culture, and society.

Recent classroom research has utilized LE to investigate the creation of translanguaging spaces in various educational settings (e.g., Mendoza, 2020; Mulvey, 2020; Zhu et al., 2020; Beiler, 2021). For instance, Zhu et al. (2020) examined how the integration of diverse linguistic and multimodal resources facilitates the formation of a translanguaging space during lessons at a multilingual karate club. This club, based in London, serves a group of multi-ethnic and multilingual children. Using LE as their methodological framework, the authors collected a variety of data sources, including field notes, video recordings of lessons, photos of the linguistic landscape, and social media data. Their analysis shows how a karate instructor creatively and critically orchestrates multilingual and multimodal repertoires to support the learning of Japanese karate terms and his teaching. Specifically, the analysis reveals that multimodal repertoires are not secondary to verbal utterances; rather, verbal utterances are used to cue and complement body movements, which become part of the multimodal repertoire. As learning and performing Japanese karate terms is emphasized equally with learning karate moves, practicing Japanese becomes an embodied performance, repeated, copied, and refined alongside the drilling of moves. Other available linguistic repertoires serve as languages of explanation, elaboration, or reinforcement. The authors conceptualized the karate club as a translanguaging space where the coach and students engage various meaning-making systems to create new configurations of language practices.

Mulvey (2020) used LE to examine how ideological orientations influence the programs and curricula of Japanese heritage language schools in the UK, as well as teachers' pedagogical practices in classroom interactions. The study focuses on two Japanese weekend schools in the UK and collects various data sources, including teacher interviews and field notes from classroom observations. The findings indicate that a monolingual ideology significantly shapes the programs and teachers' pedagogical practices in both schools. In the classrooms, although some teachers view a monolingual language policy as the preferred method for promoting L2 Japanese acquisition, their pedagogical practices allow students to use different linguistic practices to support meaning-making processes. The study argues that translanguaging serves as a positive ideological orientation for teachers, enabling them to accept heterogeneous students as they are and use these diverse language practices as a pedagogical resource. However, it is important to note that the analysis of classroom discourse was brief and lacked fine-grained detail, which limited the readers' understanding of how different linguistic resources were orchestrated to create a translanguaging space in the classrooms.

Beiler (2021) conducted a four-month linguistic ethnographic study to investigate how translanguaging is manifested in the teaching and learning of EAL for both linguistically majoritized and minoritized students in a Norwegian secondary school. The data collected included field notes, video recordings of classroom interactions, student texts and teacher-written feedback, photographs, and interviews with both teachers and students. From the analysis of translanguaging practices, Beiler identified two key themes: (1) bilingual English–Norwegian practices were more frequently observed in accelerated and mainstream settings, correlating with students' perceived proficiency in English; and (2) translanguaging involving minoritized languages was consistently marked across all three settings as a deviation from the dominant linguistic practices, thereby distinguishing majoritized (English–Norwegian) from minoritized translanguaging. This study underscores the analytical value of describing locally significant forms of translanguaging alongside the specific discourses they challenge or transcend, within the language ecologies that shape translanguaging in different classroom contexts. It emphasizes the need for both teachers and students to critically examine the language ideologies that lead them to view majoritized language practices as appropriate in school settings while regarding minoritized translanguaging – whether their own or others' – as antisocial, suspicious, or only valuable for communication within linguistically minoritized homes and social environments.

The cited studies (e.g., Zhu et al., 2020; Beiler, 2021) have addressed a research gap in the field that calls for more balanced research. This balance involves combining the micro-analysis of classroom discourse data with situating this analysis within the larger social context. The goal is to avoid providing rich descriptions of the social context without a detailed analysis of the actual discourse data. This approach further reinforces the methodological framework of LE, which does not prioritize the analysis of interactional data over other ethnographic data. Instead, all ethnographic data are integrated to illuminate the social phenomena being investigated.

### 4.1.4 Moment Analysis

Moment Analysis, proposed by Li (2011), examines the innovative language use of multilinguals during social interactions. This approach was suggested to study multilingual creativity in daily social interactions, aiming to shift the analytic focus from identifying frequent and regular linguistic patterns to spontaneous, creative actions that have both immediate and lasting impacts. Therefore, Moment Analysis concentrates on what triggered a particular action at a specific moment and the outcomes of that action, including the responses from others.

A moment can be identified by two main characteristics. First, it is both ordinary and noticeable to participants in the social interaction as well as to the analyst. It is ordinary because it naturally occurs in conversation and is not a major incident that would drastically change an individual's life. However, a moment worthy of analysis must be noticeable due to its creativity, often being directly commented on by participants either immediately or later in the interaction, or marked by a pause for reflection. The analyst's role is to understand how participants make sense of their world (Smith et al., 2013). Second, the noticeability of the moment implies procedural consequentiality, a concept from CA (Hutchby and Wooffitt, 1998), which examines if and how the context or setting of social interaction influences the shape, form, trajectory, content, or character of the social interaction. This involves observing how a creative and spontaneous use of language is recognized, adopted, and remarked upon by participants, including their reactions, and considering what prompted the specific action at that particular moment.

Moment Analysis draws on data from various sources, emphasizing the importance of both observing and recording naturally occurring interactions, along with collecting metalanguaging data, which are commentaries on speakers' language practices as they experience them. Metalanguaging data are valuable because the process of individuals making sense of their world, particularly language users reflecting on their own and others' linguistic performances, is a crucial part of their cognitive processes during the creative moment of action. These data are combined with the analyst's observations and interpretations of naturally occurring behaviour, resulting in what can be described as a double hermeneutic: the participants are trying to understand their world, and the researcher is trying to understand the participants' efforts to make sense of their world (Smith and Osborn, 2008).

Currently, there is a limited amount of research that uses Moment Analysis as the methodological approach to conceptualize multilingual classrooms as translanguaging spaces (e.g., Hirsu, 2020; Aleksic and García, 2024; Wen, 2025). Hirsu's (2020) study is one of the first studies that utilize Moment Analysis to examine how the peer-education program 'Sharing Lives, Sharing Languages' helps migrants in Scotland create translanguaging spaces. These translanguaging spaces enable migrants to explore their identities and develop new language practices to enhance their sense of belonging within the local community. The study gathered a variety of data, including observation notes, photographs from group meetings with migrants, and artefacts created by participants. Hirsu aimed to identify the critical and creative moments within the programme, with findings showing that migrants use diverse linguistic and multimodal resources to understand their shared experiences in group meetings. This process helps them form new social connections through discussion. The study argues that the program fosters translanguaging spaces, which strengthen migrants' social bonds and transform their understanding of language discrimination and linguistic inadequacy. Despite Hirsu's efforts to analyse interactional and metalanguage data, it is important to note that the study relies heavily on field notes for recording interactional data. This reliance limits the ability to conduct a detailed analysis of how translanguaging spaces are created during actual social interactions.

Aleksic and García's (2024) study employs Moment Analysis to examine how a teacher's translanguaging practices enhance children's sense of belonging in a Luxembourgish preschool, focusing on the development of this sense moment-by-moment. The research closely observed one lesson, particularly spotlighting a student named Milan, who speaks Czech, Estonian, and French but has limited knowledge of Luxembourgish. Using video interaction analysis, the authors sequentially analysed classroom video data, complemented by interviews with the teacher and Milan's parents. The study identifies seven key moments of translanguaging pedagogical interactions between the teacher and Milan, during which the teacher: (1) helps Milan develop a voice as a storyteller, (2) raises other students' awareness of multilingualism, (3) recognizes the class's multilingualism as a resource, (4) engages with students' interests, (5) elaborates on children's curiosities, (6) fosters a collaborative learning environment, and (7) nurtures Milan's identity as a Luxembourgish speaker. The analysis reveals that Milan gradually develops a sense of belonging by first forming a relationship with the teacher through smiles and brief interactions, and then slowly connecting with his peers through smiles, gestures, and eventually confidently using Luxembourgish to communicate. This suggests that the teacher's translanguaging practices play a crucial role in encouraging children to express themselves and support their cultural identities, motivating participation and fostering a positive perception of belonging. Although the study reveals the different moments of the teacher's translanguaging practices, the interviews with the teacher and parents complementing the classroom analysis are not considered metalanguaging data (Li, 2011) as they do not invite participants to comment on their use of multilingual and multimodal resources during specific moments of interaction. Nonetheless, the study has significant pedagogical implications for early childhood education, emphasizing the importance of preschool teachers adopting a positive stance towards translanguaging and engaging in practices that support children's sense of belonging in school.

Wen's (2025) study is, to the best of my knowledge, the first to employ Moment Analysis to investigate how multilinguals use translanguaging practices to foster creativity in a task-based-language-teaching classroom. Conducted at a mainland Chinese university, Wen gathered a variety of data sources, including classroom observations, stimulated-recall interviews, and artefacts. Utilizing translanguaging theory and the 5A's creativity framework, Wen identified creative comments and categorized them into broad themes. This analysis is further triangulated with participants' reflections on their own creative translanguaging practices. The findings reveal that multilinguals actively create translanguaging spaces within their groups, promoting creativity by incorporating past experiences, coordinating multilingual, multimodal, and multi-sensory resources, and expressing their multilingual identities. The study supports the idea that creativity is achieved by students through self-expression, the creation of new language practices, and their roles as co-creators of knowledge and linguistic development. Based on these findings, Wen developed a task-based-language-teaching and translanguaging-contextualized 5A's creativity framework. This framework captures how multilinguals act as agents, considering the affordances of the broader sociocultural environment, engaging in continuous interactions with audiences, and performing creative actions through translanguaging to generate new artefacts, thereby building connections with each other.

Based on the cited studies (Hirsu, 2020; Aleksic and García, 2024; Wen, 2025), it is evident that Moment Analysis allows researchers to examine translanguaging within specific temporal instances and discern the resulting consequences. This analytical approach requires both an emic perspective, achieved through the micro-analysis of specific moments, and an etic perspective, which complements the analysis with metalanguaging data collected from stimulated-recall or semi-structured interviews. In the next section, I will explain how the combination of Multimodal CA with IPA is inspired by Moment Analysis.

### 4.1.5 Integrating Multimodal Conversation Analysis with Interpretative Phenomenological Analysis

The combination of Multimodal CA with IPA is a methodological approach that is proposed by Tai (2023) with the aim of exploring the complexities of translanguaging practices in multilingual interactions. This approach is inspired by Li's (2011) concept of Moment Analysis and the use of translanguaging as an analytical perspective. The goal is to examine how language users blend different languages and non-linguistic semiotic systems during specific moments in social interactions, and to understand the triggers and consequences of these social actions. To conduct this analysis, researchers must collect video recordings of natural interactions and video-stimulated-recall-interview data, which serves as metalanguage data. This metalanguage data helps researchers better understand how language users make sense of their experiences (Li, 2011).

As outlined in Section 4.1.2, Multimodal CA investigates how social order is collaboratively constructed by members of a social group through detailed analyses of social interactions. This method avoids making prior assumptions about the relevance of language-in-use and focuses on examining sequences of interactions rather than isolated turns or utterances. However, Multimodal CA primarily analyses publicly observable actions and does not delve into participants' private thoughts or feelings. Its objective is to document the resources that speakers use to construct social actions during interactions. It is crucial to acknowledge that creating a translanguaging space is complex, influenced by various sociocultural factors such as personal history, identity, and beliefs (Li, 2011). Given that Multimodal CA alone cannot account for the impact of participants' individual histories, beliefs, and other factors in forming translanguaging spaces in classroom interactions (Tai, 2023), the IPA of video-stimulated-recall-interviews provides a deeper insight into how teachers and students perceive their translanguaging practices during specific interaction moments. Video-stimulated-recall-interviews are particularly suitable for IPA as they capture how people experience, perceive, describe, feel about, judge, remember, make sense of, and discuss a phenomenon with others (Smith et al., 2023).

The dual interpretation process in IPA, known as the 'double hermeneutic', allows researchers to interpret how participants make sense of their world. This approach requires analysts to take an emic perspective to grasp the complexities of participants' lived experiences. The second part of the hermeneutic process involves researchers interpreting participants' interpretations of their experiences, encouraging them to incorporate theoretical concepts from outside the data to explain psychological phenomena. This involves adopting an etic perspective to enhance the emic analysis of participants' lived experiences. Using an etic perspective in IPA is crucial, as it aligns with recent calls for more studies employing CDA as a methodological framework to understand classroom discourse. It has been suggested that while CA helps researchers uncover innovative practices of interactants and provides a more nuanced view of language use, its descriptive nature should be paired with a critical ideological analysis that reconnects local knowledge with dominant ideologies and power structures. This combination can contribute to understanding the effectiveness and transformative potential of translanguaging in classroom discourse (Kimura and Tsai, 2023). I contend that integrating Multimodal CA with IPA addresses Kimura and Tsai's (2023) call for combining micro-analytic findings (i.e., CA findings) with other relevant influences affecting classroom interactions. This integration reveals how classroom interaction is shaped by various factors, including institutional policies, goals, and broader social ideologies about language and knowledge.

To conduct a critical analysis of classroom talk, researchers should begin with a micro-analysis using Multimodal CA and then triangulate this with the IPA analysis of video-stimulated-recall-interview data, ensuring they maintain the analytic rigor of Multimodal CA. Additionally, researchers must be cautious when applying external theories to interpret participants' experiences. During IPA analysis, it is crucial that all interpretations are grounded in the interview data, which requires close attention to the data itself. As Smith et al. (2013, p. 37) state, a successful interpretation is one that is 'based on a reading from within the terms of text which the participant has produced'. Therefore, I argue that combining Multimodal CA and IPA offers a new analytical strategy for understanding both the processes and causes of translanguaging in the classroom.

In addition to my own research, which integrates Multimodal CA with IPA to examine translanguaging practices in various classroom settings – such as

English-Medium-Instruction mathematics classrooms (e.g., Tai and Li, 2020), English-Medium-Instruction history classrooms (e.g., Tai, 2024b), online language learning classrooms (e.g., Tai and Zuo, 2024), English-as-a-First-Language classrooms (Tai and Wong, 2023), EAL classrooms (e.g., Wong and Tai, 2023), Chinese-as-an-Additional-Language classrooms (e.g., Tai and Lee, 2024), and Information-Technology/Programming classrooms (e.g., Tai, 2024a) – other scholars have also employed this combination to uncover the complexities of translanguaging practices in classroom interactions (e.g., Xia, 2022; Putra, 2024; Wang et al., 2025).

Focusing on the pedagogical tensions in a mainland Chinese secondary school, Xia (2022) offered empirical evidence supporting the effectiveness of combining Multimodal CA with IPA for investigating L2 classroom interactions. The study examines EAL classrooms in mainland Chinese secondary schools. The Multimodal CA analysis of classroom video data reveals that the EAL teacher employs various linguistic and multimodal resources to achieve multiple pedagogical goals, such as emphasizing language points, reinforcing comprehension, and distinguishing phonetics. The IPA analysis underscores the importance of understanding contextual factors that influence teachers' translanguaging practices in classroom interactions. For instance, the teacher recognizes the practical value of translanguaging in assisting students with low L2 English proficiency. This study demonstrates the benefits of combining Multimodal CA with IPA to explore the complexities of translanguaging processes and the conflicting pressures teachers face between adhering to monolingual ideologies and addressing multilingual realities.

Shifting the focus to raciolinguistic justice, Putra (2024) investigated EAL teachers' efforts to create translanguaging spaces that empower students' linguistic and semiotic repertoires, aiming for linguistic justice and inclusion to challenge raciolinguistic ideologies. Utilizing Multimodal CA to examine classroom interaction data from an EAL classroom at an Indonesian university, and triangulating this with teachers' stimulated-recall interview data using IPA, the study identified three themes: (1) adapting language use to match students' English proficiency to facilitate classroom discussion, (2) fostering relational and critical dispositions to help students navigate various communicative contexts effectively, and (3) enabling students to utilize their semiotic repertoire to promote inclusive education. These findings illustrate how the teacher creates a translanguaging space that supports equitable and inclusive L2 English learning. The IPA analysis particularly highlights the teachers' commitment to implementing translanguaging practices, encouraging students to challenge raciolinguistic ideologies and affirm their linguistic repertoires.

A recent study by Wang et al. (2025) examined how an EAL teacher uses translanguaging to enhance students' motivation in learning L2 English and their vocabulary acquisition in a Chinese secondary school EAL classroom. Classroom video recordings were used to showcase the teacher's pedagogical strategies, while post-stimulated-recall interviews with the teacher explored perceptions of translanguaging practices from selected video clips. Additionally, focus group interviews with students were conducted to understand changes in their L2 English motivation and attitudes towards translanguaging. By integrating Multimodal CA with IPA, the findings indicate that translanguaging enables students to use their L1 for meaning-making, alleviating learning stress and fear of mistakes, which in turn boosts participation, confidence, and L2 motivation. The teacher employs multimodal resources to scaffold students' understanding of L2 vocabulary and maintain their motivation. The authors argue that the teacher's translanguaging practices significantly transformed students' L2 Motivational Self-System (L2MSS), as evidenced by a shift from an 'ought-to L2 self' to an 'ideal L2 self' (p. 26). However, the dynamic interaction between translanguaging and students' L2 motivation is not fully captured in the IPA analysis, as interviews were only conducted with the teacher, not the students. Therefore, it is crucial to gather students' metalanguaging data to understand their perceptions of translanguaging during classroom interactions and how it supports their ideal or ought-to L2 selves, as well as how it shapes their L2 learning experiences.

Thus, I argue that integrating Multimodal CA with IPA allows researchers to explore the development of translanguaging practices in multilingual classrooms and how both teachers and students perceive these practices during specific classroom interactions. This methodological approach, which emphasizes detailed analysis of social interactions (Multimodal CA) and insights into individuals' lived experiences (IPA), offers researchers a framework to combine micro-analytic findings with broader sociocultural influences, such as policies, beliefs, and ideologies. This combination is valuable for examining the opportunities and challenges of implementing translanguaging pedagogy in classroom settings.

## 4.2 Summary

This section provides a comprehensive methodological roadmap for researching translanguaging in classroom interactions, critically examining the affordances and limitations of five key approaches: CDA, which exposes how translanguaging practices intersect with power and ideology; CA, which offers a fine-grained view of how translanguaging is interactionally co-constructed in real-time; LE, which situates these micro-interactions within broader sociocultural contexts; Moment Analysis, which zooms in on consequential episodes of multilingual creativity; and the integrated use of Multimodal CA with IPA, a method the section champions for its ability to bridge the gap between observable classroom translanguaging practices and participants' own perceptions of their use of translanguaging at specific moments of the classroom interactions. By synthesizing empirical studies that employ these diverse frameworks, the section argues that a multi-methodological perspective is essential to fully capture the complexities of translanguaging – not only as a pedagogical practice but as a socially embedded and politically consequential phenomenon, thereby equipping researchers with the analytical tools to investigate its transformative potential and inherent challenges in multilingual classrooms.

## 5 Conclusion

### 5.1 Theoretical Contributions to Applied Linguistics

Research on classroom discourse has traditionally focused on spoken interaction to understand the relationship between language, learning, and teaching (Walsh, 2010). However, a translanguaging perspective demands a radical rethinking of this very concept. It compels us to see classroom discourse not merely as an exchange of spoken words within four walls, but as a dynamic, multi-semiotic flow orchestrated by teachers and students using their full multilingual and multimodal repertoires (Tai, 2024c). This flow transcends the physical classroom through digital platforms and AI, and challenges the monolingual biases embedded in traditional analysis. By examining how participants creatively blend linguistic, gestural, visual, and spatial resources to construct meaning, we move beyond a narrow view of 'talk' to understand discourse as the very fabric of a translanguaging space – a space where learning is co-constructed, power dynamics are negotiated, and students' entire communicative resources are recognized. Therefore, studying classroom discourse through a translanguaging lens is not just beneficial but essential, as it provides the critical toolset needed to understand and foster genuinely inclusive and equitable multilingual learning environments.

Research on translanguaging in multilingual classrooms has questioned the longstanding ideology of viewing languages as separate entities in traditional linguistic theories, instead proposing that meaning-making is a fluid and dynamic translanguaging process. This perspective enables teachers to utilize their complete multilingual and multimodal resources to meet their pedagogical objectives (Tai, 2023; Li, 2024). Specifically, this study makes theoretical contributions to the field of Applied Linguistics by emphasizing key themes such as: (1) translanguaging pedagogy for creating spaces that challenge institutionalized monolingualism, (2) the opportunities and challenges associated with translanguaging pedagogy, and (3) the adoption of the trans-prefix to develop new theoretical concepts.

In this Element, I have argued that translanguaging pedagogy, as distinct from pedagogical translanguaging (Cenoz and Gorter, 2021), is conceptualized as a transformative approach in language education. Researchers, such as García and Li (2014) and Li (2024), shift away from the pedagogical translanguaging model, which involves the planned use of specific named languages for particular educational objectives. Instead, translanguaging pedagogy emphasizes empowering teachers to leverage multilingual students' linguistic awareness, diverse knowledge bases, and multimodal resources to enrich classroom activities and enhance both content and language learning. In essence, translanguaging not only supports meaning-making in the classroom but also transforms the classroom into a space for students' personal translanguaging journeys. This approach allows students to integrate aspects of their lives, cultures, and linguistic knowledge creatively, ensuring that all students' lived experiences are included in the educational process. It also transforms how students perceive each other's language practices and experiences (Aleksic and García, 2024; Tai and Wong, 2024).

Researchers in the field have emphasized the importance of not only exploring the benefits of translanguaging pedagogy but also addressing its challenges in promoting social justice (e.g., Charalambous et al., 2016; Allard, 2017). Empirical studies have shown that teachers' translanguaging practices do not always facilitate student engagement due to unequal power dynamics in the classroom (e.g., Qin and Llosa, 2023; Shepard-Carey, 2023). Additionally, research (e.g., Sah and Li, 2022; Tai, 2025b) introduces the concept of 'unequal translanguaging', highlighting the limitations in teachers' translanguaging practices when they fail to utilize students' indigenous or home languages as resources to support and enhance content and language learning. This is often due to teachers' preference for national languages over indigenous languages (Sah and Li, 2022) or their unfamiliarity with students' home languages (Tai, 2025b). Therefore, in order to implement translanguaging pedagogy in classrooms, this requires teachers to consider how power and ideology are intertwined with classroom translanguaging practices. It also necessitates an understanding of how different multilingual and multimodal resources can either enable or constrain the creation of transformative translanguaging spaces that promote social justice and inclusion.

This Element has emphasized the potential of using the trans-prefix to develop new theoretical concepts, helping to reconceptualize existing ideas and deepen our understanding of the complexities of interactional phenomena. I have shown how the concept of translanguaging has inspired new theoretical constructs, such as translanguaging sub-spaces (Tai, 2023; Tai and Li, 2023), trans-semiotising (Lin, 2015; Wu and Lin, 2019), transpositioning (Li and Lee, 2024; Tai, 2025a), transmodalities (Hawkins, 2018), transknowledging (e.g., Heugh, 2021), transprogramming (Tai, 2024a), and transculturing (e.g., Lin and Chen, 2025). These concepts highlight the value of incorporating the trans-prefix into languaging (Li, 2018), which underscores fluid practices that transcend socially constructed language systems and structures, demonstrates the transformative potential of the translanguaging process for generating new identities, values and practices, and reveals the transdisciplinary impacts of rethinking learning and language use. This plays a role in bridging gaps across fields, such as linguistics, psychology, sociology, computer science, and education.

## 5.2 Methodological Contributions to the Research on Translanguaging in Classroom Discourse

To advance research in this field, we must move beyond studying translanguaging in classroom discourse and begin to conceptualize classroom discourse as translanguaging. This paradigm shift requires methodologies that treat the classroom not as a venue for pre-defined linguistic codes, but as a dynamic translanguaging space where meaning is continuously co-constructed through the integrated orchestration of multilingual, multimodal, and multi-semiotic resources. Adopting translanguaging as an analytical perspective means the primary focus is no longer on isolated languages or modes, but on the fluid, boundary-transcending process of meaning-making itself. This perspective does not prioritize any particular communication mode or method over others (Li, 2018). Crucially, surpassing boundaries between different forms of expression is a key element of translanguaging, distinguishing it from the concept of code-switching. Unlike code-switching, which concentrates on the functional aspects of language use, translanguaging acknowledges the complex nature of creating meaning through various modes of communication (Tai, 2025a). Such a perspective highlights that classroom discourse is an embodied, multi-semiotic flow where multilingual and multimodal resources are not treated as separate elements, but as interconnected threads in a single, unified communicative event.

Methodologically, adopting translanguaging as an analytical lens allows researchers to go beyond structural analyses that focus solely on common linguistic patterns. Li (2011) introduced Moment Analysis to adopt translanguaging as an analytical perspective for exploring linguistic innovation and change among multilingual individuals. This method investigates spontaneous acts of creativity and criticality in everyday interactions, focusing on what prompts a specific social action at a given moment and its subsequent effects. It emphasizes understanding how participants notice or comment on the use of various linguistic, multimodal, and multi-semiotic resources at particular moments, and what leads to these actions. Future research could benefit from the methodological approach developed by Tai (2023), which combines Multimodal CA with IPA to explore the complexities of translanguaging practices in multilingual classrooms. This analysis requires collecting diverse data, such as observational and video recordings of natural interactions, as well as metalanguage data – speakers' reflections on their language use and their employment of semiotic and modal resources. This methodological combination encourages researchers to adopt both emic (Multimodal CA and IPA) and etic (IPA) perspectives to triangulate and analyse data sources, thereby integrating micro-analytical findings with broader influences like identities, ideologies, policies, and beliefs that underlie classroom interactions. By doing so, it contributes to the ongoing effort of adopting a critical analytical approach, such as CDA, to foster a comprehensive understanding of how translanguaging can disrupt racial, linguistic, and cultural categories to promote social justice, rather than sustaining monolingual ideologies and discourses.

## 5.3 Future Research Directions

Future research on translanguaging in classroom discourse could explore several key themes: (1) the impact of translanguaging on students' content and L2 learning, creativity and criticality, and their emotional well-being, (2) utilizing Douglas Fir Group's trans-disciplinary framework for studying translanguaging in classroom interaction, (3) advancing the conceptualization of translanguaging as a significant mediator for students' L2 motivational development in learning contexts that adopt L2 as the medium-of-instruction and (4) creating an AI-mediated translanguaging space.

### 5.3.1 The Impact of Translanguaging on Students' Content and L2 Learning, Creativity and Criticality, and Their Emotional Well-Being

Future research on multilingual classroom discourse would benefit from examining the effects of translanguaging pedagogy on students' L2 and content learning, creativity, critical thinking, and emotional well-being, including aspects such as foreign language anxiety (e.g., Tai and Lee, 2024). Empirical evidence from such studies will help develop sustainable pedagogical strategies for training teachers to effectively use translanguaging in multilingual classrooms. The study of Foreign Language Anxiety (FLA) in classroom settings, which focuses on the psychological impact of learning academic content in an L2 or acquiring an additional language, is still evolving. FLA refers to the anxiety students feel in L2 classrooms, potentially leading to negative beliefs about their language proficiency and reduced self-confidence. The challenges faced by multilingual learners when studying content through an additional language can affect their emotional well-being, including a lack of self-confidence in speaking the target language in L2 or CLIL classes, and feelings of dissatisfaction with classroom teaching (Dovchin, 2021; Dryden et al., 2021). Therefore, further research is needed to investigate how EMI/CLIL/L2 teachers use translanguaging practices to reduce students' anxiety in learning content and/or L2, and to promote enjoyment, participation, and learning. It is crucial to explore students' positive emotions, such as enjoyment, as significant responses to or outcomes of EMI/CLIL/L2 teachers' pedagogical methods. To address these research gaps, I argue that enhancing teachers' ability to create translanguaging spaces in classroom interactions can support students in managing anxiety, fostering enjoyment, and encouraging participation in learning content through the target language (Tai and Lee, 2024; Tai and Wang, 2025).

### 5.3.2 Douglas Fir Group's Transdisciplinary Framework for Studying Translanguaging in Classroom Interaction

Classroom researchers are encouraged to apply the transdisciplinary framework developed by the Douglas Fir Group (DFG) (2016) to study translanguaging in classroom interactions, as recommended by Mendoza et al. (2024). This framework outlines three interconnected levels of influence on L2 acquisition: the micro-level, involving social interactions between individuals; the meso-level, encompassing institutions and communities; and the macro-level, which includes ideological structures in the wider society. The DFG emphasizes that researchers should take into account these intersecting dimensions of context, even when concentrating on one particular aspect.

(1) Micro-interactional context: This encompasses moment-to-moment interactions and semiotic resources, including linguistic, interactional, nonverbal, and visual elements.
(2) Meso-institutional context: This pertains to the 'small culture' of schools and classrooms, shaped by educational policies, program goals/design, and the dynamics of agency and power within classroom interactions.

(3) Macro-political/ideological context: This includes the language discourses, policies, ideologies, prejudices, belief systems, and values that are prevalent in the broader society.

A recent study by Tian and Lau (2023) adopted the transdisciplinary framework developed by the Douglas Fir Group (2016) to examine how various contextual factors influence the Grade 3 Mandarin teacher's translanguaging practices. At the classroom (micro) level, the teacher observed that most of her English-speaking students brought their dominant language, cultural backgrounds, and learning styles into the Mandarin learning environment. This finding aligns with Tai and Li (2020), who showed that translanguaging helps teachers connect classroom learning with students' everyday lives, making lessons more relevant. At the school (meso) level, the Chinese-English bilingual program was only a small part of the broader school context, where most staff were monolingual English speakers and did not share the teacher's positive attitudes towards multilingualism. The school's culture tended to uphold the dominant status of English, mirroring broader societal (macro-level) trends. Moreover, the emphasis on high-stakes testing and the monolingual bias present in US educational policy further limited opportunities for minoritized language development. Tian and Lau argue that multilingual teachers should strengthen their agency as critical policymakers within their classrooms and develop their skills and identities as researchers. By doing so, they can question existing practices, advocate for change, and contribute to reshaping school policies at the meso-level.

Focusing on EMI education, Tai (2025c) integrated micro-, meso-, and macro-level analyses in order to understand how the creation of a translanguaging space in EMI classrooms shapes students' translanguaging learning experience, contributes to students' language learning motivation, and facilitates their transition from a first-language medium of instruction to a new EMI environment. At the micro-level, classroom interaction analysis shows the teacher strategically orchestrating Cantonese, English, and iPad features (e.g., zooming, symbols) to clarify mathematical concepts, manage exam strategies, and boost motivation. The meso-level analysis, drawn from interviews, identifies the institutional EMI policy as a key driver, motivating the teacher to challenge monolingual approaches in order to address students' diverse needs and ease their transition from Chinese-medium primary schools. Finally, at the macro-level, the data reveals how sociocultural pressures, particularly the high-stakes examination system, strongly shape students' 'ought-to L2 self', with the teacher's translanguaging practices serving as a crucial buffer to help students cope with this pressure while navigating the demands of the EMI environment.

It is argued that students' L2 learning motivation 'is shaped not only from an individual/static perspective, but also evolves in response to, and is co-constructed with, forces at the micro-, meso-, and macro-levels within the DFG framework' (p. 23).

Thus, the DFG framework offers an ecological view on how translanguaging practices in multilingual classroom interactions are shaped by meso-level 'small cultures' created by school leaders and teachers, as well as macro-level language policies, ideologies, and broader sociocultural influences (Mendoza et al., 2024; Tai et al., 2025). It encourages researchers to study translanguaging within its context, which includes examining who holds power in the classroom. This power can stem from higher proficiency in languages that society values, more 'standard' ways of speaking these languages, greater familiarity with the academic literacies valued in the school environment, more 'legitimate' forms of translanguaging (e.g., Tai, 2025b) and/or the unequal teacher-student power dynamics in the classroom.

### 5.3.3 Conceptualizing Translanguaging as a Mediator for Students' L2 Motivational Development in Learning Contexts that Adopt L2 as the Medium-of-Instruction

There is substantial evidence indicating that translanguaging is an effective pedagogical approach for enhancing both content and language learning in L2 medium-of-instruction settings (e.g., Prada, 2021; Qin and Llosa, 2023; Tai, 2024b). Translanguaging involves teachers and students employing a variety of linguistic, semiotic, and sociocultural resources from their multilingual repertoires to facilitate meaning-making (Li, 2018). However, the potential benefits of translanguaging for developing students' L2 learning motivation remain under-explored (Wang et al., 2024). Considering the complex and dynamic nature of L2 learning motivation (LLM), the interaction between translanguaging practices and motivational development requires further investigation. In other words, understanding how L2 students learn is crucial due to the motivational challenges posed by EMI/CLIL and other target-language-only policies and practices. Transitioning from mother-tongue-based instruction to an additional-language-as-medium-of-instruction can cause many L2 students to struggle, especially those from socially disadvantaged backgrounds (e.g., Sah and Li, 2022). Not all teachers and students are adequately prepared to teach and learn content subjects through the L2, which may impede students' learning progress.

Furthermore, the DFG's transdisciplinary framework does not sufficiently address how LLM functions across these interconnected levels. Since LLM is affected by various social domains – namely macro, meso, and micro contexts – and translanguaging can influence students' LLM and identities (Hennebry-Leung and Gao, 2023), it is crucial to explore students' LLM and their experiences with translanguaging practices in classroom settings from a multi-layered perspective (Mendoza et al., 2024). To address this gap, I propose a reconceptualized framework of the L2MSS, which integrates DFG's (2016) transdisciplinary framework with Dornyei's (2009) L2MSS to guide the exploration of the role of translanguaging in enhancing students' LLM (Mendoza et al., 2024; Tai, 2025c). This contextual framework will help us better understand how EMI/CLIL/L2 students' experiences with translanguaging affect their LLM in settings where L2 is the medium of instruction. It centres on LLM, incorporating L2 self-guides (ideal and ought-to L2 selves) as key elements of student motivation. Moreover, students' L2 self-guides are shaped by their translanguaging learning experiences, reflecting various contextual factors at the micro, meso, and macro levels. Theoretically, this revised L2MSS framework will provide researchers with a comprehensive understanding of L2MSS by integrating the micro-level experiences of L2 students within broader institutional and sociocultural contexts (Tai, 2025c).

In this revised framework, I redefine the concept of 'L2 learning experience', originally from Dornyei's (2009) L2MSS framework, by introducing the idea of *translanguaging learning experience* (Tai, 2025c). This term describes the translanguaging practices that students participate in both inside and outside the classroom to support their content and language learning. Traditionally, 'L2 learning experience' refers to the motivational influence of the learning environment and experience (Dornyei, 2009), focusing solely on acquiring comprehensive knowledge of a specific named language. However, it's crucial to redefine 'L2 learning experience' as 'translanguaging learning experience', because language use is context-specific and integrated into everyday life, employing various objects and resources that enable individuals to effectively engage in interactions using the L2 (Greer and Wagner, 2023; Prada, 2025). Research in both neuropsychology and sociolinguistics has shown that language is inherently connected with other cognitive and semiotic systems in the process of meaning-making (e.g., Li, 2018). There is substantial neuro-anatomic evidence refuting the idea that different neural activations occur when a speaker uses more than one language (e.g., Thierry, 2016). The concept of translanguaging encourages viewing multilingualism as a single language system rather than multiple separate systems. Since language learning requires contextual practice, much of it happens not only in the classroom but also in diverse environments like communities and homes, where translanguaging is common (Li, 2022). Therefore, language learning is a translingual, trans-modal, and trans-sensory experience, involving students in using various linguistic structures, systems, and modalities to develop new knowledge (Zhu et al., 2020).

The reconceptualized framework recognizes that students' translanguaging learning experiences can be influenced across three dimensions: (1) *the micro-level*, where students' experiences are shaped by their own use of translanguaging in and out of the classroom, as well as by the teacher's use of translanguaging during classroom interactions; (2) *the meso-level*, which focuses on how students' experiences are affected by the school's 'small culture', such as its language policy; and (3) *the macro-level*, which involves broader sociocultural factors, including official policies, beliefs, and ideologies that influence students' translanguaging learning experiences (see Figure 1).

By exploring these interconnected layers, this revised framework aims to offer an ecological perspective on the development of students' L2 self-guides. This framework highlights the interaction between the L2 ideal and ought-to

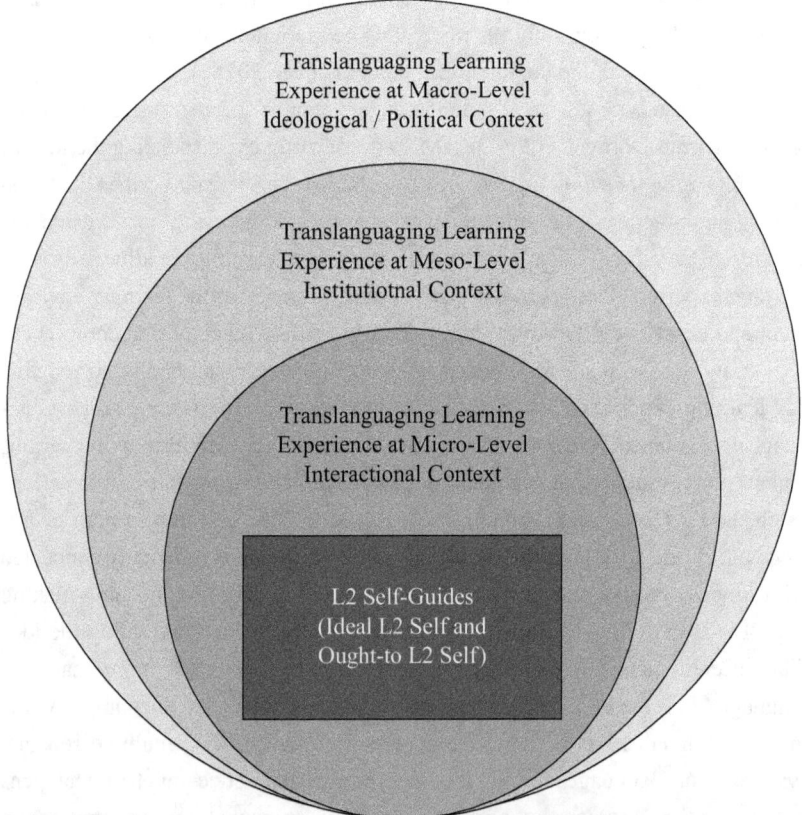

**Figure 1** A reconceptualized framework for researching translanguaging and L2 motivation in context (Tai, 2025c).

selves and students' translanguaging learning experience in order to better understand students' LLM in contexts where additional language is used as the medium-of-instruction. This framework will also provide a comprehensive understanding of LLM, enabling EMI/CLIL/L2 teachers to identify specific issues that need to be addressed and determine the levels at which these issues arise, thereby enhancing students' LLM (Tai, 2025c).

### 5.3.4 Theorizing Multilingual Classrooms as an Artificial Intelligence–Mediated Translanguaging Space

Generative AI (GenAI) refers to a form of AI that learns from human languages to create unique texts in various formats, such as written language, images, music, and videos. Most GenAI systems use large language models to detect patterns in vast amounts of text data, allowing them to produce coherent, human-like content (Liu and Zhao, 2025). However, there is limited research on human-AI interaction from a linguistic perspective. To address this gap, Tang (2025) introduced the concept of AI-textuality, which describes the 'intertextual process through which meaning is co-constructed between humans and GenAI systems, involving the interpretation, creation, and integration of AI-generated texts within a larger network of connected texts' (p. 2). This concept seeks to portray human-AI interaction as a dynamic exchange between human experiences in the physical world and GenAI's computational operations in the digital realm. Essentially, AI-textuality recognizes that entities like GenAI are not merely passive information holders but active participants that shape the way texts are accessed, understood, created, and communicated. This idea aligns with post-humanist views that emphasize the shared agency between humans and non-human entities in language and communication (e.g., Pennycook, 2017).

By conceptualizing GenAI as an active non-human contributor in the creation of new knowledge, future research can investigate how educators might incorporate GenAI to encourage multilingual students to engage in translanguaging practices. This could foster new forms of knowledge and discourse within classroom interactions. In an upcoming discussion paper, Jeon et al. (2025) explored both the potential and the limitations of GenAI in interpreting local expressions. They illustrate how translanguaging can be used as a theoretical framework to identify and address GenAI's limitations. One example provided is the Chinglish term 'departyment', which combines 'department' and 'party' to critique government departments for prioritizing social events (Li, 2018). However, ChatGPT's interpretation focuses solely on the lexical difference between 'department' and 'departyment', overlooking the socio-political context. Consequently, there is a concern that GenAI might mislead users into thinking its outputs reflect genuine societal voices, especially given that human-AI communication can mimic human-to-human interactions. To counter this, it is suggested that teachers encourage students to critically evaluate AI-generated content, assessing it for bias, ethics, and trustworthiness.

Building on the notion of technology-mediated translanguaging space that was proposed by Tai and Li (2024) and Tai (2024e), I introduce the notion of *AI-mediated translanguaging space* to theorize the nature of the translanguaging space that is created for and also created by translanguaging practices and GenAI-supported resources. Although there is increasing acknowledgment of GenAI's potential in supporting translanguaging, there remains a significant gap in the literature concerning their interaction (e.g., Tang, 2024, 2025). Addressing this gap is crucial, as understanding how GenAI can foster the creation of translanguaging spaces in classroom interactions could yield valuable insights into how multilingual individuals leverage their full linguistic and semiotic repertoires to communicate and engage across diverse spaces and modes of interaction. In classrooms characterized by linguistic and cultural diversity, teachers and students may not share the same L1 or cultural background, and teachers might lack proficiency in students' home languages as well as an understanding of their cultural contexts. This challenge is evident in classroom settings such as adult EAL classrooms in the US (Tai and Khabbazbashi, 2019a; Tai and Dai, 2024) and CAL classrooms for ethnic minority students in Hong Kong (e.g., Tai and Lee, 2024; Tai, 2025b). Such linguistic and cultural barriers can hinder students from leveraging their diverse multilingual resources, including their home or heritage languages, to articulate their understanding of language or subject matter content, which can also contribute to a lack of motivation in learning and heightened foreign language anxiety. Therefore, I argue that constructing an AI-mediated translanguaging space can empower both teachers and students to harness GenAI, thereby expanding their multilingual and multimodal repertoires. This expansion can facilitate the creation of new knowledge and enhance participation in classroom interactions.

AI-mediated translanguaging spaces offer the potential for creating a dynamic and inclusive classroom environment where linguistic and cultural diversity is not only acknowledged but actively integrated into the learning process. Through GenAI's ability to process and generate content across various languages and modes, teachers and students can access resources that better reflect their linguistic and cultural backgrounds, lived experiences and funds of knowledge (Lin and Chen, 2025; Lo, 2025). This translanguaging space encourages a more holistic engagement with L2 and content learning, enabling students to navigate complex linguistic landscapes and participate more fully in classroom discussions. By bridging linguistic gaps, AI-mediated translanguaging spaces can transform educational practices, fostering an environment where all students feel valued and empowered to contribute to the collective learning experience.

## 5.4 Summary

This Element has argued that adopting translanguaging as an analytical perspective fundamentally reconfigures our understanding of classroom discourse, transforming it from a channel for the exchange of pre-defined linguistic codes into a dynamic, collaborative process co-constructed through the integrated orchestration of students' and teachers' full multilingual and multimodal repertoires. By conceptualizing a classroom as a translanguaging space, I reframe classroom discourse itself as the very medium through which power is negotiated, knowledge is co-constructed, and students' identities are affirmed. This theoretical shift necessitates robust methodological approaches, like combining Multimodal CA with IPA, to fully capture the complexities of this fluid meaning-making process. Ultimately, viewing classroom discourse through a translanguaging lens is not merely an analytical choice but an ethical imperative which provides the essential theoretical and methodological frameworks for understanding how teachers can create genuinely equitable, inclusive, and transformative multilingual learning environments for our students.

# References

Aleksić, G., and García, O. (2024). A Multilingual Preschooler's School Belonging: The Role of Translanguaging Pedagogy. *Journal of Language, Identity & Education*, 1–23.

Allard, E. C. (2017). Re-Examining Teacher Translanguaging: An Ecological Perspective. *Bilingual Research Journal*, 40(2), 116–130.

Allwright, R. L. 1980. "Turns, Topics, and Tasks: Patterns of Participation in Language Learning and Teaching." In D. Larsen-Freeman (ed.) *Discourse Analysis in Second Language Research*. (pp. 165–187). Rowley, MA: Newbury House Publishers.

Anderson, J. (2024). Translanguaging: a paradigm shift for ELT theory and practice. *ELT Journal*, 78(1), 72–81.

Antaki, C. (2012). What actions mean, to whom, and when. *Discourse Studies*, 14, 493–498.

Ashton, J. R. (2015). Keeping up with the class: A critical discourse analysis of teacher interactions in a co-teaching context. *Classroom Discourse*, 7(1), 1–17.

Atar, C., & Rafi, A. S. M. (2024). Classroom interaction in an online context: A translanguaging informed conversation analysis perspective. *International Journal of Educational Development*, 105, 102970.

Baker, C. (2001). *Foundations of bilingual education and bilingualism* (3$^{rd}$ edition). UK: Multilingual Matters.

Baker, C. (2011). *Foundations of bilingual education and bilingualism*. UK: Multilingual Matters.

Baker, W., and Sangiamchit, C. (2019). Transcultural Communication: Language, Communication and Culture Through English as a Lingua Franca in a Social Network Community. *Language and Intercultural Communication*, 19(6), 471–87.

Bao, R., and X. Du. (2015). Implementation of Task-based Language Teaching in Chinese as a Foreign Language: Benefits and Challenges. *Language, Culture and Curriculum*, 28(3), 291–310.

Bauman, Z. (2012[2000]). *Liquid modernity*. Cambridge: Polity.

Beiler, I. (2021). Marked and unmarked translanguaging in accelerated, mainstream, and sheltered English classrooms. *Multilingua*, 40(1), 107–138.

Bengochea, A., Sembiante, S. F., & Gort, M. (2020). Exploring the object-sourced transmodal practices of an emergent bilingual child in sociodramatic play. *Journal of Early Childhood Research*, 18(4), 371–386.

Bonacina-Pugh, F. (2012). Researching "Practiced Language Policies": Insights from Conversation Analysis. *Language Policy*, 11, 213–234.

Bozbiyik, M., and Morton, T. (2025). Connecting target content with students through translanguaging in a postgraduate EMI pharmacology module. *Journal of Multilingual and Multicultural Development*, 46(7), 1815–1832.

Brantmeier, E. J. (2013). Pedagogy of vulnerability: Definitions, assumptions, and applications. In J. Lin, R. Oxford, & E. J. Brantmeier (Eds.), *Re-envisioning higher education: Embodied pathways to wisdom and transformation* (pp. 95–106). Charlotte, NC: Information Age.

Cenoz, J. (2017). Translanguaging in school context. International perspectives: An introduction. *Journal of Language, Identity and Education*, 16, 193–1–98.

Cenoz, J. and Gorter, D. (2017). Sustainable translanguaging and minority languages: Threat or opportunity? *Journal of Multilingual and Multicultural Development*, 38, 901–12.

Cenoz, J., and Gorter, D. (2021). *Pedagogical translanguaging*. Cambridge: Cambridge University Press.

Charalambous, P., Charalambous, C., and Zembylas, M. (2016). Troubling translanguaging: Language ideologies, superdiversity and interethnic conflict. *Applied Linguistics Review*, 7, 327–352.

Cheshire, J., and Fox, S. (2009). 'Was/were variation: A perspective from London'. *Language Variation and Change*, 21, 1–38.

Cook, V., & Li, W. (Eds.). (2016). *The Cambridge handbook of linguistic multicompetence*. Cambridge: Cambridge University Press.

Copland, F., and Creese, A. (2015). *Linguistic Ethnography: Collecting, Analysing and Presenting Data*. London: SAGE.

Cowley S. J. (2017). Changing the idea of language: Nigel Love's perspective. *Language Sciences*, 61, 43–55.

Coyle, D., Hood, P., and Marsh, D. (2010). *CLIL: Content and language integrated learning*. Cambridge: Cambridge University Press.

Curry, RM and Cunningham, P. (2000). Co-learning in the community. *New Directions for Adult and Continuing Education*, 2000(87), 73–82.

Davies, B., and Harré, R. (1990). Positioning: The discursive production of selves. *Journal for the Theory of Social Behaviour*, 20(1), 43–63.

de los Rios, C. and Seltzer, K. (2017). Translanguaging, coloniality, and English classrooms: An exploration of two bicoastal urban classrooms. *Research in the Teaching of English*, 52(1), 55–76.

Dörnyei, Z. (2009). 'The L2 Motivational Self System'. In Z. Dörnyei and E. Ushioda (eds.), *Motivation, Language Identity and the L2 Self*, (p. 9–42). Bristol: Multilingual Matters.

Douglas Fir Group. (2016). A Transdisciplinary Framework for SLA in a Multilingual World. *The Modern Language Journal*, 100, 19–47.

Dovchin, S. (2021). Translanguaging, emotionality, and English as a second language immigrants: Mongolian background women in Australia. *TESOL Quarterly*, 55(3), 839–865.

Dryden, S., Tankosic, A., and Dovchin, S. (2021). Foreign language anxiety and translanguaging as an emotional safe space: Migrant English as a foreign language learners in Australia. *System*, 101, Article 102593.

East, M., and Wang, D. (2025). Advancing the communicative language teaching agenda: what place for translanguaging in task-based language teaching? *The Language Learning Journal*, 53(6), 702–714.

Fairclough, N. 2013. *Language and Power*. London: Routledge.

Flanders, N. A. (1970). *Analyzing Teaching Behavior*. Reading, Mass: Addison Wesley Pub. Co.

Flores, N. (2020). From Academic language to language architecture: Challenging raciolinguistic ideologies in research and practice. *Theory into Practice*, 59(1), 22–31.

Ford, C. (2012). Clarity in applied and interdisciplinary conversation analysis. *Discourse Studies*, 14, 507–513.

Galante, A. (2020). Pedagogical translanguaging in a multilingual English program in Canada: Student and teacher perspectives of challenges. *System*, 92, 1–16.

García, O., and W, Li. (2014). *Translanguaging: Language, bilingualism and education*. Basingstoke: Palgrave Macmillan.

García, O., Flores, N., Seltzer, K., Wei, L., Otheguy, R., & Rosa, J. (2021). Rejecting abyssal thinking in the language and education of racialized bilinguals: A manifesto. *Critical Inquiry in Language Studies*, 18(3), 203–228.

García, O., Johnson, S., & Seltzer, K. (2017). *The translanguaging classroom. Leveraging student bilingualism for learning*. USA: Caslon.

Greer, T., and Wagner, J. (2021). The interactional ecology of homestay experiences: Locating input within participation and membership. *Second Language Research*, 39(1), 85–113.

Gu, M., Lee, C. and Jin, T. (2023). A translanguaging and trans-semiotizing perspective on subject teachers' linguistic and pedagogical practices in EMI programme. *Applied Linguistics Review*, 14(6), 1589–1615.

Hamman-Ortiz, L., Dougherty, C., Tian, Z., Palmer, D., & Poza, L. (2025). Translanguaging at School: A Systematic Review of U.S. PK-12 Translanguaging Research. *System*, 129, 103594

Han, X., Li, W., & Filippi, R. (2022). The effects of habitual code-switching in bilingual language production on cognitive control. *Bilingualism: Language and Cognition*, 25(5), 869–889.

Hawkins, M. (2018). Transmodalities and Transnational Encounters: Fostering Critical Cosmopolitan Relations. *Applied Linguistics*, 39(1), 55–77.

Hawkins, M. R. (2022). 'Global storybridges: Being and becoming'. In M. R. Hawkins (ed.) *Transmodal Communications: Transpositioning Semiotics and Relations*, (pp. 1–21). Clevedon: Multilingual Matters.

Hennebry-Leung, M. and Gao, X. (2023). *Language learning motivation in a multilingual Chinese context*. London: Routledge.

Heritage, J. (1995). Conversation analysis: methodological aspects. In U. M. Quasthoff (ed.). *Aspects of oral communication*, (pp. 391–418). Berlin/New York: Walter de Gruyter.

Heugh, K. (2021). Southern multilingualisms, translanguaging and transknowledging in inclusive and sustainable education. In P. Harding-Esch & H. Coleman, *Language and the Sustainable Development Goals.*, (pp. 33–43). London: British Council.

Heugh, K., French, M., Arya, V., Pham, M., Tudini, V., Billinghurst, N., Tippett, N., Chang, L.-C., Nichols, J., & Viljoen, J.-M. (2022). Multilingualism, translanguaging and transknowledging: Translation technology in EMI higher education. *AILA Review*, 35(1), 89–127.

Hirsu, L. (2020). Lessons in response-ability: supporting social encounters by 'doing' language. *Language and Intercultural Communication*, 20(2), 153–166.

Ho, W. Y. J. (2022). The construction of translanguaging space through digital multimodal composing: A case study of students' creation of instructional videos. *Journal of English for Academic Purposes*, 58, 101134.

Ho, W. Y. J., and Tai, K. W. H. (2024). Translanguaging in digital learning: the making of translanguaging spaces in online English teaching videos. *International Journal of Bilingual Education and Bilingualism*, 27(9), 1212–1233.

Hutchby, I., and Wooffitt, R. (1998). *Conversation Analysis: Principles, practices and applications*. Malden, MA: Blackwell.

Jacknick, C. M. (2011). Breaking in is hard to do: how students negotiate classroom activity shifts. *Classroom Discourse*, 2(1), 20–38.

Jakonen, T., Szabó, T. P., and Laihonen, P. (2018). Translanguaging as playful subversion of a monolingual norm in the classroom. In G. Mazzaferro (ed.). *Translanguaging in everyday practice*, (p. 31–48). Singapore: Springer.

Jenks, C. J. (2020). Applying Critical Discourse Analysis to Classrooms. *Classroom Discourse*, 11(2), 99–106.

Jeon, J., Lee, S., Tai, K. W. H., and Li, W. (2025). Generative AI and Its Dilemmas: Exploring AI from a Translanguaging Perspective. *Applied Linguistics*, 46(4), 709–717.

Jewitt, C. (2014). An introduction to multimodality. In Jewitt, C. (Ed.), *The Routledge Handbook of Multimodal Analysis*, (pp. 15–30). London: Routledge.

Jørgensen, M., and Phillips, L. J. (2002). Critical discourse analysis. In *Discourse Analysis as Theory and Method* (pp. 60–95). London: SAGE.

Kasper, G. (2001). Classroom research on interlanguage pragmatics. In K. R. Rose & G. Kasper (Eds.), *Pragmatics in language teaching*. (pp. 33–60). New York: Cambridge University Press.

Kimura, D., and Tsai, A. (2023). Decolonizing classroom discourse: insights from interactional research. *ELT Journal*, 77(3), 327–337.

Kress, G. 1997. *Before Writing: Rethinking the Paths to Literacy*. London: Routledge.

Ladson-Billings, G. (1995). But that's just good teaching! The case for culturally-relevant pedagogy. *Theory Into Practice*, 34, 159–165.

Lee, Y. 2007. Third turn position in teacher talk: contingency and the work of teaching. *Journal of Pragmatics*, 39(6), 1204–1230.

Lefebvre, H. (1991). *The production of space*. Oxford: Blackwell.

Lemke, J. L., & Lin, A. M. Y. (2022). Translanguaging and flows: Towards an alternative conceptual model. *Educational Linguistics*, 1(1), 134–151.

Leonet, O., Cenoz, J. and Gorter, D. (2020). Developing morphological awareness across languages: Translanguaging pedagogies in third language acquisition. *Language Awareness*, 29, 41–59.

Lewis, G., Jones, B., & Baker, C. (2012). Translanguaging: Origins and development from school to street and beyond. *Education Research and Evaluation*, 18(7), 641–654.

Li, W. (2011). Moment analysis and translanguaging space: Discursive construction of identities by multilingual Chinese youth in Britain. *Journal of Pragmatics*, 43, 1222–1235.

Li, W. (2014). Negotiating funds of knowledge and symbolic competence in the complementary school classrooms. *Language and Education*, 28(2), 161–180.

Li, W. (2016). 'Multi-competence and the translanguaging instinct'. In Cook, V., and Li W. (eds): *The Cambridge handbook of multi-competence*. Cambridge: Cambridge University Press, 533–43.

Li, W. (2018). Translanguaging as a practical theory of language. *Applied Linguistics*, 39, 9–30.

Li, W. (2020). Multilingual English users' linguistic innovation. *World Englishes*, 39, 236–248.

Li, W. (2021). Translanguaging as a political stance: Implications for English language education. *ELT Journal*, 76(2), 172–182.

Li, W. (2022). Translanguaging as method. *Research Methods in Applied Linguistics*, 1(3), 100026.

Li, W. (2024). Transformative pedagogy for inclusion and social justice through translanguaging, co-learning, and transpositioning. *Language Teaching*, 57(2), 203–214.

Li, W., and Lee, T. K. (2023). Transpositioning: Translanguaging and the liquidity of identity. *Applied Linguistics*, 45(5), 873–888.

Li, W., and Lin, A. M. Y. (2019). Translanguaging classroom discourse: pushing limits, breaking boundaries. *Classroom Discourse*, 10(3–4), 209–215.

Li, W., and Zhu, H (2013). Translanguaging Identities and Ideologies: Creating Transnational Space Through Flexible Multilingual Practices Amongst Chinese University Students in the UK. *Applied Linguistics*, 34(5), 516–535.

Li, W., & García, O. (2022). Not a First Language but One Repertoire: Translanguaging as a Decolonizing Project. *RELC Journal*, 53(2), 313–324.

Liu, G. L., and Zhao, X. (2025). The predictive effects of sociobiographical variables, English learning confidence, and digital competence on AI-mediated informal digital learning of English (AI-IDLE). *International Journal of Applied Linguistics*, 1–12.

Lin, A. M. Y. (2015). Egalitarian Bi/Multilingualism and Trans-Semiotizing in a Global World. In W. E. Wright, S. Boun, and O. García (Eds.), *The Handbook of Bilingual and Multilingual Education* (pp. 19–37). West Sussex, UK: Wiley Blackwell.

Lin, A. M. Y., and He, P. (2017). Translanguaging as Dynamic Activity Flows in CLIL Classrooms. *Journal of Language, Identity & Education*, 16(4), 228–244.

Lin, A. M. Y., and Wu, Y. (2015). 'May I speak Cantonese?' – Co-constructing a scientific proof in an EFL junior secondary science classroom. *International Journal of Bilingual Education and Bilingualism*, 18(3), 289–305.

Lin, A. M. Y., and Chen, Q. (2025) Towards Ethical and Responsible Engagement of Generative AI in Education: The PAA Model and 4T Lenses in Action'. In F. V. Lim and J. Pun (eds.), *Designing Learning with Multimodality in English Medium of Education (EME) Classrooms Across Asia* (pp. 235–58). London: Bloomsbury.

Lin, S., & Leung, A. (2024). ESL classroom interactions in a translanguaging space. *Applied Linguistics Review*, 15(6), 2397–2425.

Liu, Y. (2020). Translanguaging and trans-semiotizing as planned systematic scaffolding: Examining feeling-meaning in CLIL classrooms. *English Teaching & Learning*, 44(2), 149–173.

Lo Bianco, J. (2007). Emergent China and Chinese: Language Planning Categories. *Language Policy*, 6(1), 3–26.

Lo, A. W. T. (2025). Culture travellers: Theorizing transculturing through transcultural fandom in the GenAI age. *Applied Linguistics*, 1–26.

Love, N. (1990). The locus of languages in a redefined linguistics. In: Davis, Hayley G., Taylor, Talbot J. (Eds.), *Redefining Linguistics*. London: Routledge, 53–117.

Lu, C., Gu, M. M., & Lee, J. C. K. (2023). A systematic review of research on translanguaging in EMI and CLIL classrooms. *International Journal of Multilingualism*, 22(2), 1033–1053.

Macaro, E. (2018). *English Medium Instruction*. Oxford: Oxford University Press.

Markee, N. (2005). Conversation analysis for second language acquisition. In E. Hinkel (ed.). *Handbook of research in second language teaching and learning*, (p. 355–374). Mahwah, NJ: Lawrence Erlbaum.

Markee, N. (1995). Teachers' answers to students' questions: problematizing the issue of making meaning. *Issues in Applied Linguistics*, 6(2), 63–92.

Matsumoto, Y. (2018). At challenging but "learning" moments: Roles of non-verbal interactional resources for dealing with conflicts in English as a lingua franca classroom interactions. *Linguistics and Education*, 48, 35–51.

Mendoza, A. (2022). What does translanguaging-for-equity really involve? An interactional analysis of a 9th grade English class. *Applied Linguistics Review*, 13(6), 1055–1075.

Mendoza, A., Hamman-Ortiz, L., Tian, Z., Rajendram, S., Tai, K. W. H., Ho, W. Y. J., and Sah, P. (2024). Sustaining Critical Approaches to Translanguaging in Education: A Contextual Framework. *TESOL Quarterly*, 58(2), 664–692.

Moll, L, Amanti, C., Neff, D., & Gonzalez, N. (1992). Funds of knowledge for teaching: Using a qualitative approach to connect homes and classrooms. *Theory into Practice*, 31(2), 132–141.

Moorhouse, B. L., Walsh, S., Li, Y., & Wong, L. (2022). Assisting and mediating interaction during synchronous online language lessons: Teachers' professional practices. *TESOL Quarterly*, 56(3), 934–960.

Morell, T. (2007). What enhances EFL students' participation in lecture discourse? Student, lecturer and discourse perspectives. *Journal of English for Academic Purposes*, 6(3), 222–237.

Mulvey, N. (2021). Translanguaging as ideology: Responding to social and linguistic diversity in the classroom of Japanese as a heritage language schools in England. *Journal of Asian Pacific Communication*, 31(2), 236–259.

Nikula, T., and Moore, P. (2019). Exploring translanguaging in CLIL. *International Journal of Bilingual Education and Bilingualism*, 22(2), 237–249.

Nikula, T., Jakonen, T., & Käänta, L. (2024). Multimodal practices of unpacking and repacking subject-specific knowledge in CLIL physics and chemistry lessons. *Learning and Instruction*, 92, Article 101932.

Nystrand, M. (1997). *Opening Dialogue: Understanding the Dynamics of Language and Learning in the English Classroom*. New York: Teachers College Press.

Ollerhead, S. (2019). Teaching across semiotic modes with multilingual learners: translanguaging in an Australian classroom. *Language and Education*, 33(2), 106–122.

Otheguy, R., García, O., and Reid, W. (2015). Clarifying translanguaging and deconstructing named languages: A perspective from linguistics. *Applied Linguistics Review*, 6(3), 281–307.

Ou, W. A., and Gu, M. M. (2022). Competence beyond language: translanguaging and spatial repertoire in teacher-student interaction in a music classroom in an international Chinese University. *International Journal of Bilingual Education and Bilingualism*, 25(8), 2741–2758.

Paulsrud, B., Tian, Z., & Toth, J. (Eds.) (2021). *English-Medium Instruction and Translanguaging*. Bristol, UK: Multilingual Matters.

Pennycook, A. (2017) *Posthumanist Applied Linguistics*. New York: Routledge.

Prada, J. (2019). Exploring the role of translanguaging in linguistic ideological and attitudinal reconfigurations in the Spanish classroom for heritage speakers. *Classroom Discourse*, 10(3–4), 306–322.

Prada, J. (2025). A translanguager's take on a synergy-driven SLA/T. *The Modern Language Journal*, 109(1), 116–118.

Psathas, G. (1995). *Conversation analysis: The study of talk-in-interaction*. CA: Sage.

Putra, H. S. (2024). Teacher Agency in Reproducing Translanguaging Practices as Social Justice Strategy to Decolonize ELT. *IAFOR Journal of Education*, 12(3), 203–242.

Qin, K. and Llosa, L. (2023). Translingual caring and translingual aggression: (Re)centering criticality in the research and practice of translanguaging pedagogy. *The Modern Language Journal*, 107(3), 713–733.

Radke, S. C., Vogel, S., Hoadley, C., and Y., J. (2020). Representing Percents and Personas: Designing Syncretic Curricula for Modeling and Statistical

Reasoning. *The Interdisciplinarity of the Learning Sciences: Conference Proceedings*, 3, 1365–72.

Rafi, A. S. M., and Morgan, A. M. (2023). Blending translanguaging and CLIL: pedagogical benefits and ideological challenges in a Bangladeshi classroom. *Critical Inquiry in Language Studies*, 20(1), 20–45.

Rajendram, S. (2023). Translanguaging as an agentive pedagogy for multilingual learners: affordances and constraints. *International Journal of Multilingualism*, 20(2), 595–622.

Rajendram, S., Shi, W., & Jun, J. (2023). Translanguaging in higher education: experiences and recommendations of international graduate students from the Global South. *Critical Inquiry in Language Studies*, 20(3), 258–278.

Rampton, B. (2007). Neo-Hymesian linguistic ethnography in the United Kingdom. *Journal of Sociolinguistics*, 11(5), 584–607.

Rampton, B., Tusting, K., Maybin, J., Barwell, R., Creese, A., and Lytra, V. (2004). UK linguistic ethnography: a discussion paper. Available from www.ling-ethnog.org.uk

Ruiz de Zarobe, Y., and Querol-Julián, M. (2025). Multilingualism and multimodality in the CLIL/EMI classroom. *Journal of Multilingual and Multicultural Development*, 46(5), 1397–1415.

Richards, K. (2003). *Qualitative Inquiry in TESOL*. Basingstoke: Palgrave Macmillan.

Richards, K. (2006). Being the teacher: Identity and classroom conversation. *Applied Linguistics*, 27(1), 51–77.

Sah, P., and Li, G. (2022). Translanguaging or unequal languaging? Unfolding the plurilingual discourse of English medium instruction (EMI) in Nepal's public schools. *International Journal of Bilingual Education and Bilingualism*, 25(6), 2075–2094.

Seals, C., & Olsen-Reeder, V. (2020). Translanguaging in conjunction with language revitalization. *System*, 92, Article 102277.

Seedhouse P. (2004). *The interactional architecture of the language classroom: a conversation analysis perspective*. London: Blackwell.

Seltzer, K. (2019). Reconceptualising home and school language: Taking a critical translingual approach in the English classroom. *TESOL Quarterly*, 53(4), 986–1007.

Sembiante, S. F., Bengochea, A., & Gort, M. (2025). Morning circle as a community of practice: Co-teachers' transmodality in a dual language bilingual education preschool classroom. *Journal of Early Childhood Literacy*, 25(2), 283–307.

Sert, O. (2015). *Social Interaction and Classroom Discourse*. UK: Edinburgh University Press.

Sert, O., and Walsh, S. (2012). The interactional management of claims of insufficient knowledge in English language classrooms. *Language and Education*, 27(6), 542–565.

Shepard-Carey, L. (2023). Creating space for translingual sensemaking: a critical discourse analysis of teacher translanguaging during small-group reading. *Classroom Discourse*, 14(4), 344–365.

Sidnell, J. (2010). *Conversation analysis: An introduction*. UK: Wiley Blackwell.

Sinclair, J., and Coulthard, R. M. (1975). *Towards an analysis of discourse: the English used by teachers and pupils*. London: Oxford University Press.

Smith, J. A., Flowers, P., and Larkin, M. (2013). *Interpretative phenomenological analysis: Theory, method, and research*. CA: Sage.

Song, Y. (2024). Translanguaging as decoloniality-informed knowledge co-construction: a nexus analysis of an English-Medium-Instruction program in China. *Applied Linguistics Review*, 15(2), 713–736.

Swain, M. (2006). Languaging, agency and collaboration in advanced second language proficiency. In H. Byrnes (ed.). *Advanced Language Learning: The Contribution of Halliday and Vygotsky*. (pp. 95–108). London: Continuum.

Tai, K. W. H. (2022). Translanguaging as Inclusive Pedagogical Practices in English Medium Instruction Science and Mathematics Classrooms for Linguistically and Culturally Diverse Students. *Research in Science Education*, 52(3), 975–1012.

Tai, K. W. H. (2023). *Multimodal Conversation Analysis and Interpretative Phenomenological Analysis: A Methodological Framework for Researching Translanguaging in Multilingual Classrooms*. London: Routledge.

Tai, K. W. H. (2024a). Transprogramming in the primary-level programming lessons: Reconceptualising translanguaging in the era of artificial intelligence. *Applied Linguistics*, 1–34.

Tai, K. W. H. (2024b). Cross-curricular connection in an English Medium Instruction Western History classroom: A translanguaging view. *Language and Education*, 38(3), 435–464.

Tai, K. W. H. (2024c). Transcending the Boundaries of Mode in Online Language Teaching: A Translanguaging Perspective on ESL Teachers' Synchronous Small Group Online Tutorials. *System*, 121, 1–45.

Tai, K. W. H. (2024d). Shaping student responses into academic expressions: Analysing an English medium instruction history classroom from a translanguaging perspective. *International Journal of Bilingual Education and Bilingualism*, 27(4), 550–580.

Tai, K. W. H. (2024e). Classroom Interactional Competence in an English Medium Instruction Mathematics Classroom: A Creation of a Technology-Mediated Translanguaging Space. *Learning and Instruction*, 90, 1–21.

Tai, K. W. H. (2024f). Documenting Students' Conceptual Understanding of Second Language Knowledge: A Translanguaging Analysis of Classroom Interactions in a Primary English as a Second Language Classroom for Linguistically and Culturally Diverse Students. *Applied Linguistics Review*, 15(6), 2775–2822.

Tai, K. W. H. (2025a). Transpositioning in English Medium Instruction Classroom Discourse: Insights from a Translanguaging Perspective. *Language and Education*, 39(4), 965–999.

Tai, K. W. H. (2025b). Unequal Translanguaging in Chinese as an Additional Language Classrooms: The Affordances and Limitations of a Translanguaging Space for Supporting Ethnic Minority Students in Managing Foreign Language Anxiety. *Applied Linguistics Review*, 16(6), 2627–2671.

Tai, K. W. H. (2025c). Transitioning from Primary Chinese-Medium-Instruction to Secondary English-Medium-Instruction: The Role of Translanguaging in Contributing to EFL Students' Language Learning Motivation. *International Journal of Applied Linguistics*, 1–29.

Tai, K. W. H. (2025d). Funds of Knowledge for Synchronous Online Language Teaching: A Translanguaging View on an ESL Teacher's Pedagogical Practices. *International Review of Applied Linguistics in Language Teaching*, 63(1), 569–616.

Tai, K. W. H. and Brandt, A. (2018). Creating an Imaginary Context: Teacher's Use of Embodied Enactments in Addressing a Learner's Initiatives in a Beginner-Level Adult ESOL Classroom. *Classroom Discourse*, 9(3), 244–266.

Tai, K. W. H. and Dai, D. (2024). Observing a Teacher's Interactional Competence in an ESOL Classroom: A Translanguaging Perspective. *Applied Linguistics Review*, 15(5), 2061–2096.

Tai, K. W. H. and Khabbazbashi, N. (2019a). Vocabulary Explanations in Beginning-level Adult ESOL Classroom Interactions: A Conversation Analysis Perspective. *Linguistics and Education*, 52, 61–77.

Tai, K. W. H. and Khabbazbashi, N. (2019b). The Mediation and Organisation of Gestures in Vocabulary Instructions: A Microgenetic Analysis of Interactions in a Beginning-level Adult ESOL Classroom. *Language and Education*, 33(5), 445–468.

Tai, K. W. H., and Lee, T. K. (2024). Mitigating ethnic minority students' foreign language anxiety through co-learning in Chinese as an additional language classrooms: A transpositioning perspective. *System*, 127, 1–27.

Tai, K. W. H. and Li, W. (2020). Bringing the Outside In: Connecting Students' Out-of-School Knowledge and Experience through Translanguaging in Hong Kong English Medium Instruction Mathematics Classes. *System*, 95, 1–32.

Tai, K. W. H. and Li, W. (2021a). Co-Learning in Hong Kong English Medium Instruction Mathematics Secondary Classrooms: A Translanguaging Perspective. *Language and Education*, 35(3), 241–267.

Tai, K. W. H. and Li, W. (2021b). Constructing Playful Talk through Translanguaging in the English Medium Instruction Mathematics Classrooms. *Applied Linguistics*, 42(4), 607–640.

Tai, K. W. H. and Li, W. (2023). Embodied Enactment of a Hypothetical Scenario in an English Medium Instruction Secondary Mathematics Classroom: A Translanguaging Approach. *Language Teaching Research*, Epub ahead of Print.

Tai, K. W. H. and Li, W. (2024). The Affordances of iPad for Constructing a Technology-Mediated Space in Hong Kong English Medium Instruction Secondary Classrooms: A Translanguaging View. *Language Teaching Research*, 28(4), 1501–1551.

Tai, K. W. H., and Li, W. (2025). Engaging students in learning and creating different translanguaging sub-spaces in Hong Kong English Medium Instruction history classrooms. *Language and Education*, 39(1), 190–231.

Tai, K. W. H., Li, W., and Loh, E. K. Y. (2025). Enhancing Students' Content and Language Development: Implications for Researching Multilingualism in CLIL Classroom Context. *Learning and Instruction*, 96, 102083.

Tai, K. W. H. and Wang, X. (2025). Exploring Ethnic Minority Students' Perspectives on Anxiety in Learning Chinese as an Additional Language: An Interpretative Phenomenological Analysis. *Journal of Multilingual and Multicultural Development*, 46(10), 3868–3886.

Tai, K. W. H. and Wong, C. Y. (2023). Empowering Students Through the Construction of a Translanguaging Space in an English as a First Language Classroom. *Applied Linguistics*, 44(6), 1100–1151.

Tai, K. W. H. and Zuo, M. (2024). The Development of an ESL Teacher's Ability in Constructing a Virtual Translanguaging Space in Synchronous Online Language Tutorials. *Linguistics and Education*, 83, 1–34.

Tam, H. W.-Y. (2025). Co-constructing orthographic mediated space through Sinographic visualization in Hong Kong Chinese-as-an-additional-language classroom interactions. *Applied Linguistics*, 1–32.

Tang, K. S. (2025). AI-textuality: Expanding intertextuality to theorize human-AI interaction with generative artificial intelligence. *Applied Linguistics*, 1–19.

ten Have, P. (2007). *Doing conversation analysis (2nd Edition)*. London: Sage.

Tharp, R.G. and Gallimore, R. (1988). *Rousing Minds to Life: Teaching, Learning, and Schooling in Social Context*. Cambridge: Cambridge University Press.

Thibault P. J. (2017). The reflexivity of human languaging and Nigel Love's two orders of language. *Language Sciences*, 61, 74–85.

Thibault, P. J. (2011). First-order languaging dynamics and second-order language: The distributed language view. *Ecological Psychology*, 23, 210–245.

Thierry, G. (2016). Questions of multi-competence: a written interview. In V. Cook & L. Wei (Eds.), *The Cambridge Handbook of Linguistic Multi-Competence* (pp. 521–532). Cambridge: Cambridge University Press.

Tian, J. (2024). Co-constructing translanguaging space to facilitate participation in a novice CFL classroom. *Chinese Language and Discourse*, 15(2), 188–217.

Tian, Z., & Lau, S. M. C. (2022). Translanguaging Flows in Chinese Word Instruction: Potential Critical Sociolinguistic Engagement with Children's Artistic Representations of Chinese Characters. *Pedagogies: An International Journal*, 17(4), 282–302.

Tian, Z., & Lau, S. M. C. (2023). Translanguaging Pedagogies in a Mandarin-English Dual Language Bilingual Education Classroom: Contextualised Learning from Teacher-Researcher Collaboration. *International Journal of Bilingual Education and Bilingualism*, 26(8), 960–974.

Tian, Z., & Li Wei. (2024). Translanguaging and EFL Teaching. In G. Noblit (Ed.), *Oxford Research Encyclopedia of Education*. Oxford University Press.

Tian, Z., & Rafi, A. S. M. (2023). Centering southern perspectives in translanguaging research. *Critical Inquiry in Language Studies*, 20(3), 205–213.

Tsui, A.B.M. (1985). Analyzing Input and Interaction in Second Language Classrooms. *RELC Journal*, 16(1), 8–32.

Tusting, K., and Maybin, J. (2007). Linguistic ethnography and interdisciplinarity: Opening the discussion. *Journal of Sociolinguistics*, 11(5), 575–583.

Vogel, S., Hoadley, C., Ascenzi-Moreno, L., Menken, K. (2019). The Role of Translanguaging in Computational Literacies: Documenting Middle School Bilinguals' Practices in Computer Science Integrated Units. *Proceedings of the 50th ACM Technical Symposium on Computer Science Education*, 76, 1164–70.

Vogel, S., Hoadley, C., Castillo, A. R., & Ascenzi-Moreno, L. (2020). Languages, literacies and literate programming: can we use the latest theories on how bilingual people learn to help us teach computational literacies? *Computer Science Education*, 30(4), 420–443.

Vygotsky, L. S. (1978). *Mind in society: The development of higher psychological processes*. Cambridge, MA: Harvard University Press.

Wang, D. (2014). *English in the Chinese Foreign Language Classroom*. Frankfurt am Main: Peter Lang.

Wang, D. (2019). Translanguaging in Chinese foreign language classrooms: students and teachers' attitudes and practices. *International Journal of Bilingual Education and Bilingualism*, 22(2), 138–149.

Wang, D. (2023). Translanguaging as a social justice strategy: the case of teaching Chinese to ethnic minority students in Hong Kong. *Asia Pacific Education Review*, 24, 473–486.

Wang, X., Xia, C., Zhao, Q. & Chen, L. (2025). Enhancing second language motivation and facilitating vocabulary acquisition in an EFL classroom through translanguaging practices. *Applied Linguistics Review*, 16(5), 2183–2216.

Waring, H. Z. (2009). Moving Out of IRF: A Single Case Analysis. *Language Learning*, 59(4), 796–824.

Waring, H. Z. (2011). Learner Initiatives and Learning Opportunities in the Language Classroom. *Classroom Discourse*, 2(2), 201–218.

Walsh, S. (2010). Editorial. *Classroom Discourse*, 1(2), 101–103.

Wen, Y. (2025). Unpacking multilingual learners' creativity in the TBLT classroom: a translanguaging perspective. *Journal of Multilingual and Multicultural Development*, 46(10), 3778–3796.

Weninger, C. (2020). Investigating ideology through framing: a critical discourse analysis of a critical literacy lesson. *Classroom Discourse*, 11(2), 107–128.

Williams, C. (1994). *An evaluation of teaching and learning methods in the context of bilingual secondary education*. PhD thesis, University of Wales, Bangor.

Williams, C. (1996). Secondary education: Teaching in the bilingual situation. In Williams, C., Lewis, G., & Baker, C. (Eds.), *The language policy: Taking stock* (pp. 39–78). Llangefni, UK: CAI.

Wong, C. Y. and Tai, K. W. H. (2023). "I made many discoveries for myself": The Development of a Teacher Candidate's Pedagogical Knowledge of Translanguaging. *System*, 116, 1–16.

Wong, C. Y. C., & Tian, Z. (2025). Maximizing students' content and language development: The pedagogical potential of translanguaging in a Chinese immersion setting. *Learning and Instruction*, 95, Article 102023.

Wu, Y., and Lin, A. M. Y. (2019). Translanguaging and trans-semiotising in a CLIL biology class in Hong Kong: whole-body sense-making in the flow of knowledge co-making. *Classroom Discourse*, 10(3–4), 252–273.

Xia, L. (2022). Translanguaging as a pedagogical practice in a Chinese EFL classroom. *Asian Journal of English Language Teaching*, 31, 109–137.

Xiao, G. (2025). Rethinking translanguaging: (Trans)bordering, spatiality, and academic discourse socialization in a graduate TESOL classroom. *Applied Linguistics*, 1–24.

Zhang, H., Wang, Y., Zhou, X., Mao, W. & Xie, Q. (2025). Translanguaging for the construction of instructional immediacy in a Mandarin–Japanese crosslinguistic class. *Applied Linguistics Review*, 16(3), 1153–1176.

Zhang, J., J. Ruan, and C. Leung. (2015). *Chinese Language Education in the United States*. Dordrecht: Springer.

Zheng, Y., and Qiu, Y. (2024). Epistemic (in)justice in English medium instruction: transnational teachers' and students' negotiation of knowledge participation through translanguaging. *Language and Education*, 38(1), 97–117.

Zhou, X., Li, C., and Gao, X. (2021). Towards a Sustainable Classroom Ecology: Translanguaging in English as a Medium of Instruction (EMI) in a Finance Course at an International School in Shanghai. *Sustainability*, 13 (19), 10719.

Zhu, D., and Wang, P. (2024). A bibliometric analysis of research trends in multilingualism in English medium instruction: towards translanguaging turn. *International Journal of Multilingualism*, 22(2), 1011–1032.

Zhu, H., Li, W., & Jankowicz-Pytel, D. (2020). Translanguaging and embodied teaching and learning: lessons from a multilingual karate club in London. *International Journal of Bilingual Education and Bilingualism*, 23(1), 65–80.

Zhu, H., Li, W., and Lyons, A. (2017). Polish shop(ping) as translanguaging space. *Social Semiotics*, 27, 411–433.

Zuo, M. (2025). Navigating for Positive Group Dynamics Through Emotion Regulation: A Multimodal Conversation Analysis on Teacher Discussions in Chinese EFL Curriculum Development. *The Asia-Pacific Education Researcher*, 1–18.

Zuo, M., & Walsh, S. (2023). Translation in EFL teacher talk in Chinese universities: a translanguaging perspective. *Classroom Discourse*, 14(2), 128–146.

# Acknowledgments

First and foremost, I would like to extend my heartfelt thanks to Prof. Zhu Hua and Prof. Li Wei for their constructive feedback and unwavering patience throughout this process. Special appreciation goes to Prof. Josh Prada and Prof. Zhongfeng Tian, whose invaluable ideas and insights have greatly contributed to this book. I am also deeply grateful to my PhD students at The University of Hong Kong, Ms. Karen C. K. Choi and Ms. Xinyi Wang, for their exceptional support.

I would like to take this opportunity to thank my friends and colleagues who have been mentally supporting me throughout my academic journey. In particular, I am thankful to Dr. Miaomiao Zuo, Prof. Alex Ho-Cheong Leung, Dr. Hugo Wing-Yu Tam, Dr. Guangxiang Leon Liu, Dr. Rina Lai, Ms. Josephine Yim, Ms. Nicole Tavares, Dr. Synthia S. W. Fung, Ms. Shirley Chun Yin Tse, Prof. Chin-Hsi Lin, Mr. Alexander F. Tang, Mr. Renxiang Tian, Dr. Mingdan Wu, Dr. Yi Wang, Ms. Alice Lam, Dr. Harry Chi Hang Cho, Dr. Xuran Han, Dr. Seongyong Lee, Dr. Nasia Kotsiou, Ms. Alice T. L. Tam, and Mr. Charles S. K. Wong. Their support has meant a great deal to me.

Finally, I could not be more thankful to my parents, Mr. Derrick Tai and Ms. Stephanie Kwong, who fully supported me to pursue my dream as a Professor.

The research for this book project was supported by the General Research Fund, Research Grants Council of Hong Kong, University Grants Committee [grant number: 17620024], the Early Career Scheme, Research Grants Council of Hong Kong, University Grants Committee [grant number: 27616923], and the Teaching Development and Language Enhancement Grant 2025-2028, University Grants Committee [grant number: 020300640.910000.10000.100.01].

Cambridge Elements

# Applied Linguistics

## Li Wei
*University College London*

Li Wei is Chair of Applied Linguistics at the UCL Institute of Education, University College London (UCL), and Fellow of Academy of Social Sciences, UK. His research covers different aspects of bilingualism and multilingualism. He was the founding editor of the following journals: *International Journal of Bilingualism* (Sage), *Applied Linguistics Review* (De Gruyter), *Language, Culture and Society* (Benjamins), *Chinese Language and Discourse* (Benjamins) and *Global Chinese* (De Gruyter), and is currently Editor of the *International Journal of Bilingual Education and Bilingualism* (Taylor and Francis). His books include the *Blackwell Guide to Research Methods in Bilingualism and Multilingualism* (with Melissa Moyer) and *Translanguaging: Language, Bilingualism and Education* (with Ofelia Garcia) which won the British Association of Applied Linguistics Book Prize.

## Zhu Hua
*University College London*

Zhu Hua is Professor of Language Learning and Intercultural Communication at the UCL Institute of Education, University College London (UCL) and is a Fellow of Academy of Social Sciences, UK. Her research is centred around multilingual and intercultural communication. She has also studied child language development and language learning. She is book series co-editor for *Routledge Studies in Language and Intercultural Communication* and *Cambridge Key Topics in Applied Linguistics*, and Forum and Book Reviews Editor of *Applied Linguistics* (Oxford University Press).

## About the Series

Mirroring the Cambridge Key Topics in Applied Linguistics, this Elements series focuses on the key topics, concepts and methods in Applied Linguistics today. It revisits core conceptual and methodological issues in different subareas of Applied Linguistics. It also explores new emerging themes and topics. All topics are examined in connection with real-world issues and the broader political, economic and ideological contexts.

# Cambridge Elements

# Applied Linguistics

## Elements in the Series

*Kongish: Translanguaging and the Commodification of an Urban Dialect*
Tong King Lee

*Metalinguistic Awareness in Second Language Reading Development*
Sihui Echo Ke, Dongbo Zhang and Keiko Koda

*Crisis Leadership: Boris Johnson and Political Persuasion during the Covid Pandemic*
Philip Seargeant

*Writing Banal Inequalities: How to Fabricate Stories Which Disrupt*
Edited by Hannah Cowan and Alfonso Del Percio

*New Frontiers in Language and Technology*
Christopher Joseph Jenks

*Multimodality and Translanguaging in Video Interactions*
Maria Grazia Sindoni

*A Semiotics of Muslimness in China*
Ibrar Bhatt

*Narrative and Religion in the Superdiverse City*
Stephen Pihlaja

*Trans-studies on Writing for English as an Additional Language*
Yachao Sun and Ge Lan

*Investigating Plagiarism in Second Language Writing*
Jun Lei and Guangwei Hu

*Discourse, Materiality and Agency within Everyday Social Interactions*
Dariush Izadi

*Translanguaging in Classroom Discourse*
Kevin W. H. Tai

A full series listing is available at www.cambridge.org/EIAL

For EU product safety concerns, contact us at Calle de José Abascal, 56–1°, 28003 Madrid, Spain or eugpsr@cambridge.org.

www.ingramcontent.com/pod-product-compliance
Lightning Source LLC
LaVergne TN
LVHW011848060526
838200LV00054B/4238